THE MARTIAL ARTS

To the memory of
Master ANZAWA Heigiro

MICHEL RANDOM

Photography by
Anne-Marie and Michel Random

Translated by Judy Boothroyd

THE
MARTIAL
ARTS

English language edition first published 1978 by
Octopus Books Limited
59 Grosvenor Street
London W1

Editorial adviser to the English language edition:
Eric Dominy

First published 1977 by
Fernand Nathan Editeur
75680 Paris
France

English translation © 1978 Octopus Books Limited

© 1977 Fernand Nathan Editeur

ISBN 0 7064 0809 8

Produced by Mandarin Publishers Limited
22a Westlands Road
Quarry Bay, Hong Kong

Printed in Hong Kong

Contents

Foreword

The Martial Arts cannot be practised as a form of entertainment or distraction. They are a serious undertaking which does not necessarily mean a sad one — far from it. You cannot approach them tentatively with your fingertips, with a mere touch of the lips, or with superficial layers of thought or heart. It would be better never to become involved, but if you do, it is essential to carry on to the end, until one's being is regenerated to the point of being made man again — a real man. As soon as your naked feet have entered a Dojo, you have entered forever. If you give up, if you waver, you risk finding yourself weaker than before. An important risk and a handicap which is difficult to compensate for.

He who seeks, finds. The genuine Masters do exist; I have known some very great ones during the past thirty years. Michel Random writes about them and illustrates them excellently, his courage, his perseverance, his love of truth have opened up, for our pleasure, those doors most closed in the Martial Arts schools. His artistry, his poetry, his talent did the rest. I have actually seen the emotion of a great Japanese Master of Budo, whose eyes filled with tears at some of the subtle and mystic passages of Random's photography. He squeezed my arm without speaking a word: we looked at each other in a silent communion. In my opinion there could be no greater homage.

Such a message of beauty and truth from the East brings, I believe, an understanding which is new because it is timeless, to all those (and they are many) who are drawn and fascinated by the virile and knightly Way of Budo.

Jean-Lucien Jazarin
President of the National College of Black Belts
France

Preface

What is man's driving force? This is the sort of question which spans a lifetime and probably beyond. Having asked the question, the replies come naturally. A friend once lent me a book which was the account of man's encounter with the arrow and what resulted from it: *Zen in the Chivalrous Art of Bowmanship* by Eugen Herrigel. It related the experience of a Westerner, a German philosopher teaching in Tokyo in 1923, who wanted to understand Zen beyond what he found in books, and his meeting with a master of kyudo called Awa.

I in turn had occasion to stay in Tokyo in October 1968. I went there to produce a film and possibly to find Herrigel, the master. Awa had been dead for some time but I was introduced to the great master of kyudo in Japan, a man called Anzawa. He was 81 years old.

The master received us warmly in his small house. However, when the introductions were over, my interpreter soon turned to me in amazement: although she was Japanese and born in Tokyo, she could not understand the master's archaic language. In order to try and overcome this paradoxical situation, I tried to explain to the master how much I had gained from reading a small book, the author of which was called Herrigel. On hearing this name, the face of the master suddenly lit up. He went off to look for a photograph album and I soon realized that he had also been Herrigel's master, had recognized his talent and had fond memories of this first European student.

This was one of the events which was to enable me to return to Tokyo a year later to produce two films: *The Martial Arts of Japan* and *Shinto or the Way of the Gods*. Meanwhile, Master Anzawa had come to Europe for the first time in his life and we had been able to meet under exceptional circumstances.

I did not have an opportunity to see him again. When I returned to Japan, the master was seriously ill and was to die on 5 February 1970 at the age of 83. However, the advice he had given me and doubtless his blessing too caused me to meet friends and helpers who assisted greatly in my work. It had been an exceptionally enriching experience spiritually. Not that good fortune came daily but because throughout numerous difficulties, the intangible thread of reality was enhanced by people and contacts, the memory of whom is still intensely present. In this book, you will find the faces of masters, knowing whom has sometimes resembled a growing awareness of another human dimension or more simply, of people whose goodness, knowledge and self-effacement prove that, whatever people say, the Spirit of budo is not dead in Japan.

A book, even a film, cannot accurately portray a life lived. Rather, they provide an invitation to cross the threshold of visible techniques and definitions, for every practical experience in life leads to spiritual unity, or a simplification and clarity unifying the person, his knowledge and his power.

By that very fact, one can only speak of such a unity in terms of its expression in the form of a revelation and a gift from within, all the more unfailing because the ego has been effaced and the essence of the being has become in a way eclipsed, freed from fear, constraint, reason, all the average man's many restraints.

Budo, like all wise things, constitutes the application of the basic energy of the universe. This energy is one and knows no bounds. To be a part of it, even a very small part, enables one to understand that this energy is also an alchemy, transforming and transmuting everything it touches.

It is well known that Westerners have always needed to understand reason and analyse things with a critical approach. Qualities which quickly become unyielding obstacles when one is restricted by them. How can a man who is always agitated inside hear the silence? What is there left to learn if one believes that a certain discipline is in itself the finality of everything, or if one's body and soul, the practical and the spiritual, are opposed, if one believes in keeping for oneself all that is given, if an idea received is like a wall obscuring the horizon?

All teaching presupposes a gradual progression by degrees and stages, but it leads nowhere. The object is to reach the point where the mutation occurs, where movement generates movement, where man becomes his own master. That is why all traditional education puts the emphasis on the practical, avoiding verbal explanation for quite understandable reasons.

In this case, what is the meaning of the search for efficiency at all costs? Such debates in which black and white are opposed overlook the fact that the body is one and that one cannot speak of real efficiency without true mastership of body and soul. As soon as this mastership is more or less achieved, the person realizes for himself the sense of the journey and the search. All discussions are superfluous.

Modern myths about superman, the invincible wrecker, constitute a dangerous temptation to stretch the energy bow to the point at which the string snaps, where the being literally explodes within. Even if such beings become commercial idols, objects of public acclaim, they are nevertheless still inarticulate puppets brought to life with artificial power and energy, who inevitably turn on each other because they have not been assimilated in real terms. Energy is what one makes of it. It can be a source of life or a source of death, of creation or destruction. There is no wisdom exclusive to budo and budo does not escape universal wisdom in which finality is neither retraction nor the drying up of the intellect but its totality and harmony. To be in this sense means to know, and to know is to add energy to energy, life to life, love to love. Such is the way of the universe.

This is why one finds in this book and in all those which recognize real teaching, the same idea expressed in different ways: *hard* practice (the learning of essential techniques) must be combined with *soft* practice, just as movement is the expression of life. The moment a practice becomes one-sided, a barrier goes up and sooner or later an accident will occur.

Budo expresses life. Therefore, a number of masters adapt the teaching they receive and create new principles of their own. A synthesis such as this leads more often to purification, clarity and an understanding of the basic substance, rather than an increase in the number of techniques. Furthermore, if many masters practise different skills in life, like those of the sword and the staff, judo, karate, archery, aiki-do, etc., it is because they are above all anxious to discover the same basic principles in each one. The great tree of tradition has a trunk and fixed roots but the branches express both life and progress.

In this book, we have attempted to portray the tree, its roots and its branches and to illustrate each part separately, yet without losing sight of their fundamental integrity. However, it is difficult to go beyond the threshold. If, when the book has been read, fresh questions come to mind and the reader wants to know more, we will have achieved our aim because the purpose of this book is to show that there is a great deal to be sought and a great deal to be found out.

Michel Random

Japan from the age of the

Shinto or the Way of the gods

gods to the age of man

Shinto or the Way of the gods

Japan can be described in a word: continuity. Primitive, feudal and modern Japan are infinitely dissimilar, yet these different periods are united by sacred bonds. A single progression, one lineage lost in the origins of time seem to make these islands, far removed from other cultures, into a land chosen by the gods, a land where the gods continue to dwell.

Japan in fact has the unique privilege of being the only country where the ruling emperor belongs to a single dynasty. This dynasty, known to go back almost 2000 years is then lost in mythology relating it directly to the gods Izanagi and Izanami, creators of all that exists in Japan: the land and the people. Furthermore, this empire is still a theocracy. The emperor, a direct descendant of the kami, is the first Shinto priest of Japan. He offers the early fruits of the rice harvest to the Sun Goddess Amaterasu. This takes place in small temples built for the purpose in the gardens of the imperial palace; and it is there that the emperor invokes the blessings of the kami on Japan. Moreover, the emperor is descended from Amaterasu, the greatest divinity of the Shinto pantheon; at least, the dynasty of Jinmu-tenno, first mythical emperor of Japan, is related to her.

The emperor's direct and unbroken ancestral line was certainly at the root of all the other lines which influence the different aspects of Japanese philosophy (religion, art, war). In this way, ancient traditions have come down to us through the centuries shrouded in a secret which still often exists. Be that as it may, the Japanese ruler embodies the identity of the function and the man.

This rock which hangs in the centre of the Futenmangu cave near Naha (Okinawa) is a kami: the kami dragon of the sea.

Haniwa

Terracotta pottery, occasionally decorated, arranged in rows on a burial tumulus (kofun) or round a holy place (from the 3rd to the 7th centuries) some representing Shinto priests or warriors.

A lake on Hokkaido.

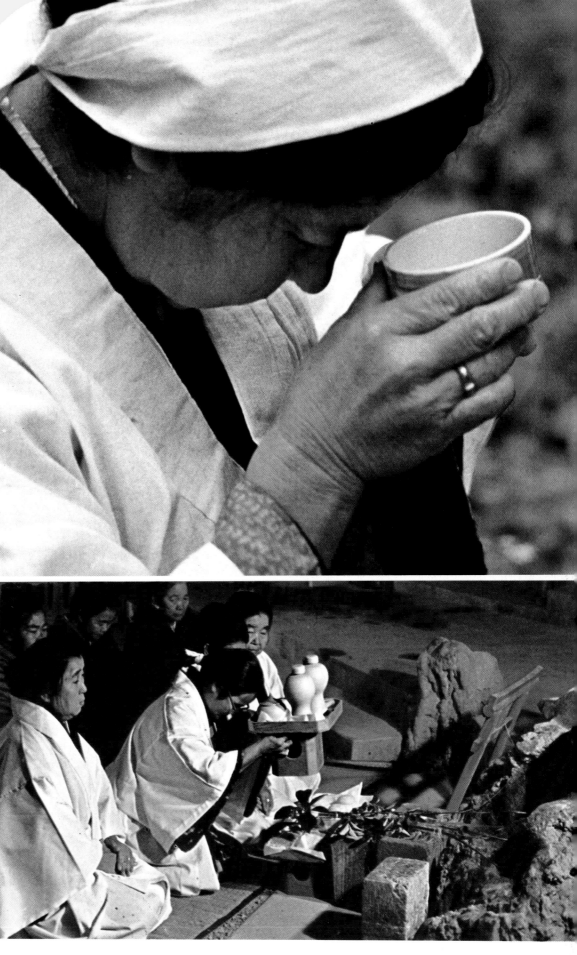

THE REVERENCE OF NATURE AND ANCIENT SHINTO

Ancient Shinto rites were practised by noro or priestesses. The noro worship the kami in natural surroundings such as caves, rocks and on cliff tops, by offering up rice and sake (an alcoholic drink made from rice).

So, to cite just one example, the guji (or great priest) of Mount Aso (Japan's largest volcano) is also called Aso and officiates in the temple of Mount Aso. His family have been priests for the past 2000 years. Mountain, temple and priest are all one. It is here that one begins to appreciate the power and magic of the old Shinto religion, and where the meaning of the Japan of today emerges.

The word 'Shinto' means 'the Way of the gods' or 'the path determined by the gods'. It is made up of the words *shin*: 'the gods', and *to*: 'the path' or 'way' (unlike Western languages, Japanese allows several words to be run together without prepositions). The word first appears in Japan in the 6th century. In the face of the emerging influence of Buddhism, it was considered necessary to define the old religion, hence the name Shinto which was given to all the ancestral practices, as opposed to Butsudo, or 'Way of Buddha'.

An empress gave the job of collecting all the traditions and legends concerning the history of Japan or Yamato to a man with a prodigious memory. The *Kojiki* or 'account of ancient matters' which became the Bible of Shinto was thus born. The *Kojiki* itself was completed eight years later by the *Nihongi,* a sort of chronicle of Japan of immeasurable value to our knowledge of the primitive beliefs of the Japanese people.

Still today, the belief of every Japanese person is founded largely on Shinto, even if he practises another religion or calls himself an atheist. This pervading spirit which exists in every Japanese person would appear to be something quite independent of itself.

For the Japanese, Shinto belongs to the group of beliefs considered by their followers

The Shinto temple at Ise lies in the heart of an ancient forest. There is no place more holy in Japan. It has been destroyed and entirely rebuilt every 20 years since the 9th century and is a symbol of purity and renewal. Shinto priests or kannushi making their way to the temple at Ise (*left*).

Shinto sanctuaries and holy places are always signalled by porticos or tori where, according to legend, the cockerel, the Sun Goddess's favourite animal, used to perch.

The torii at Itsuku Shim lead to the Itsukushima sanctuary, built in 811 on the island of Miyajima. (*right*)

to have been born simultaneously with the people, that is with the human race as a whole, in particular the people who practise them, as opposed to more exact religions such as Christianity, Buddhism and Islam, which have one founder and which have therefore come into existence at a specific time.

To define Shinto accurately in Western terms would seem to be impossible. The best way is to say that Shinto essentially defines family relationships – family relationships between men of our generation and men of more ancient generations, going back a long way, as far as the gods, since the Japanese consider that men are biologically the progeny of the gods, that is to say born of the gods.

The Kami and all things venerable

The word 'gods' is inaccurate: the correct expression is kami. It is extremely difficult for us Westerners to understand what a kami really is. The word cannot be satisfactorily translated into our language. Kami means 'that which is above' (above mankind). Let us say that all that exists is worthy of veneration and that kami encompasses all that is venerable. Izanagi and his wife Izanami, the divine couple who created the world and mankind, are kami. A mountain, a waterfall, a tree can all be kami, so can an exceptional man; a great warrior can also become kami after his death. This polytheism is confusing for us and our immediate reaction is to classify Shinto as one of the numerous animistic religions, which would be quite wrong.

The kami enable the Japanese person to feel at home with nature as a whole: mountains, rivers, clouds passing by are all his cousins. As the kami gave birth to all that exists by a purely biological process, so man himself is

Dance of Suzano-Wo.

It is here at Izumo that Suza no wo, a false god, expelled from the celestial plain, came down to earth. There he met an elderly couple who were weeping. Their eighth daughter was to be devoured by a dragon the very next day.
In exchange for the girl, Suza no wo promised to fight the dragon. He intoxicated it with a vat of sake and cut off its head.

Matsuri

In Japan, there are countless festivals or matsuri to pay hommage to the kami.

Mount Fuji

A symbol of Japan and the most sacred of mountains, Mount Fuji rises to 12,389 feet (3776 m). Its graphic shape, entirely covered in snow during winter, has been the theme of numerous illustrations. The mountain is surrounded by Shinto sanctuaries. Up to the Meiji era, a century ago, women were not permitted to climb her. Today, vast crowds go to visit her every year between June and October.

19

biologically descended from the same primordial gods. In turn, any thing or any existing being can, in so far as it accomplishes its form, become a kami. To accomplish one's form means to fulfil the essential part of one's inherent potential.

So, any tree can be a kami. However, a thousand-year-old or a several hundred-year-old tree can reveal its kami nature more precisely and be revered for it. Similarly, a man who has during his lifetime shown extraordinary qualities or virtues can become a kami upon his death and have a temple raised in his honour. There is therefore a hierarchy of the kami.

In general, Shinto is considered to be a secular religion. To a large extent, the Japanese spirit puts God aside while retaining the divorce from material limitations. So much so that the metaphysical notion which is so prominent in our monotheist religion is not apparent in the Shinto religion currently practised by 80 million Japanese. As a rule, only priests and scholars relate to the metaphysical principles of Shinto, while the average Japanese prefers to confine his interests to what he can perceive and sense directly.

Yet, this metaphysical, even esoteric framework is acutely present. In fact, the divine couple, Izanagi and Izanami, rank only eighth in the order of the creation. The first seven steps lead back to the Absolute Creator: the Master of the Centre of the Sky and, this time, the definition is identical to our meaning of the expression Creator of the Universe. These steps embrace a certain number of terrestrial kami which form the basis of the kami universe. The study of these ancient divinities (mikoto) and of the kami which followed them before the advent of Buddhism in Japan (about 538) constitutes Ko-Shinto or ancient Shinto.

As though to accentuate the assertion in the Shinto religion which requires man to keep in touch with what is at the heart of the matter the gods of fertility – water, air and fire – have been worshipped for more than nine centuries in a holy cave on the island of Okinawa.

Offerings are made to the kami: sake, water, rice, vegetables, fruit, cakes, salt, and fish.

Here and now

Here lies a fundamental characteristic and doubtless one of the secrets to understanding Japan. The Western spirit is dualistic because it worships one God, the spiritual as opposed to the worldly; the Japanese spirit on the contrary has no conception of dualism – it attains one by way of many; the principle and the form are identical; there can be no opposition between them. The two significant words of Shinto are: here and now. It is the principle of immanence as opposed to our transcendance. Instead of stressing the opposition between the weak nature of man and the intangible divinity of God, the emphasis is on the relationships between man and God. There is no spiritual aspiration but equation of the divine to man and man to the divine.

Shinto sanctuary at Kibitsu

The architecture of Shinto sanctuaries is very beautiful; the timbers are assembled without nails and cross at roof level to form an open scissors shape. These crossed timbers are reminiscent of the antlers which used to mark the home of the miyatsuko or chief medicine man.

These two women priests praying before the small Shinto altar at Naha symbolize ancient and modern Shinto.

Misogi at Kamakura

Purification rites are the very essence of the Shinto religion. These men and women renew their strength eight days every year by prayer and meditation. After breathing exercises they enter the ice-cold winter water.
The regenerating ritual bathing purifies both body and soul. When they come out of the water, men and women shake hands vigorously, signifying in spiritual terms the shaking of the soul, uniting it with the sky and the earth.

It is no doubt also why Shinto, in revering numerous kami, provides an extremely simple cult; temples which unlike all other religions of the world are very bare and stark, made of simple wood, paper and stone (on the other hand, an element of display taken from Buddhism is introduced on special occasions). The same simplicity can also be found in religious education without any form of theology or dogma.

The Shinto philosophy expressed in the book of mythology, the *Kojiki* (written in 712) stresses above all the recognition of the harmony of the universe and man's identity with the universe. This harmony embraces all matter, both animate and inanimate, the visible and the invisible. It is the principle of identity which man is invited to explore.

Harmony with nature

Here again, a different train of thought emerges. In Shinto, there are no moral restrictions, no definition of good and evil. It would take a long time to imagine the meaning and implications of such a declara-

tion; let us say that Shinto worships nature and that, in so far as man is in harmony with nature, he can only do good. To do evil therefore means cutting oneself off from nature, wishing to harm oneself, like a child who might have the power to sever the umbilical cord while still in his mother's womb. In other words, good is natural and if evil forces impede the good, one must cleanse oneself of the bad elements and do what is necessary to rid oneself of them.

In Shinto, life is a constant progression and this progression expresses the harmonious and universal order of nature which leads to unity beyond all apparent phenomena and dualistic doctrines, unity being synonymous with accomplishment and perfection. Good is the result of this unity or harmony; evil is a break and inbalance in it.

Renewal and purification

Two key words in Shinto emerge: renewal and purification. The renewal is engraved in the changing wind of the seasons. It is rejoicing at the start of a new year. The countless New Year ceremonies, celebrated in 100,000 Shinto temples in Japan (20,000 of which belong to nonorthodox sects), give rise to magnificent festivals where people flock in their millions. On New Year's Eve, at the Omiwa temple near Nara, the faithful come to seek the holy flame. Like everything, the flame must be renewed each year because, in the image of man it has accumulated all the impurities during the year. So, at Omiwa, Shinto priests go into the mountains where, by rubbing two pieces of wood together, they create a spark which is enough to light the virgin flame. The faithful come in thousands to seek this holy flame carrying small candles in bamboo dishes. When they get home they relight all the flames in the house. Similarly, all the decoration in the temples, the previous year's toys and many personal effects are burnt in different temples on vast bonfires. All around, children beat the ground with large sticks, turning and shouting to frighten off the evil which comes out of the fire.

The holy fortune tellers had a considerable influence on ancient Shinto. This fortune teller at the temple of Kibitsu is called Asome, or the pure woman. She takes her predictions from the sounds emitted by water boiling in a pot.

The eternal and the progressive

It is not by chance that Shinto attaches little importance to the existence of different continents. Beneath these continents, hidden under the sea, drifts the land which is common to islands and continents alike. This land is the symbol of duration, the foundation of eternity or at least the continuity of things. And that is why that immutable institution, the imperial family, exists in Japan.

On the other hand, more than any other civilization, Japan has cultivated this feeling of transience, represented in popular mythology by the myth of the giant sheatfish which is found under the islands of the Japanese archipelago, or 'floating world'. From there comes this sentiment of the precarious existence of living things and this contempt of death. It would appear that the fact that the word revolution has the meaning of change also stems from this idea. On this unstable planet subject to earthquakes, typhoons and natural disasters from all fronts, life must continue come what may. As an entity, Japan, land of the gods, invests the life of each individual. The inevitable death of every one, or self-sacrifice of his own identity, is a hommage to the gods.

So, Japan has no personal destiny. Her destiny is created by the form which reality

Kibitsu sanctuary. In the foreground, strips of paper or O'Harai, which when shaken from side to side play a part in the purification in all Shinto temples.

assumes. A great Shinto priest, Yamakage, said, 'To be a saint in Japan, one must have a great influence on real life.' No doubt that is why the spirit of Japan has always been to assimilate cultures and sciences whatever their origin (Chinese, Korean, or Western) without losing the essential part of its own traditions. The dawn of the 21st century will soon break on a country which scarcely more than a hundred years ago lived in feudal times.

It is therefore the union of the eternal with the progressive, a continuing process. The history of Japan is also the history of the permanent and the ephemeral in so far as these words reveal the underlying sense of the renewal and the purification.

Many emperors have changed the capital in order to rebuild it from scratch elsewhere. A number of temples and castles in Japan have been destroyed by fire and exact replicas

These priests dressed in white, the Shinto colour, are bowing devoutly in the avenue of the gods, during the annual procession at the temple of Ise.

constructed on many occasions. It is this idea of renewal which led in about 800 to an imperial decree that from then on the holiest of Shinto sanctuaries, the temple of Ise, reserved for imperial worship only, would be reconstructed in an identical form every 20 years. Recently, the sanctuary has been taken down and rebuilt for the sixtieth time. The wood from it was used to make amulets. The rebuilding of the sanctuary is an event which concerns the whole of Japan. The trees must come from a forest kept for this specific purpose and prohibited for any other use. These trees are ceremoniously felled and transported amidst popular festivities which accompany them throughout the journey.

Its outward appearance is one of summary construction but the Ise sanctuary represents an ancient form of architecture which would not have survived but for this holy practice of reconstruction. Teams of carpenters who

know the old secrets of cutting wood are trained and retained for this sole purpose. At least once in his lifetime every Japanese makes a pilgrimage to Ise. However, he cannot enter the sanctuary. Only a few visitors who deserve special recognition are lead before the holy door of the main sanctuary and may bow to it from a distance of about 11 yards (10m).

There the holy mirror is kept which Amaterasu, Goddess of the Sun, to whom the temple is dedicated, gave to the first kami who descended to earth in order to reign: Ninigi no Mikoto. It is said that an emperor who considered himself unworthy of possessing the mirror in his palace asked one of his daughters to roam Japan with the mirror until Amaterasu herself indicated the place where she wished to rest. Twenty-five years later the emperor's daughter died and another took over. After 50 years of travelling,

27

Amaterasu eventually indicated Ise, a place magnificently surrounded by forests, and it has remained there to this day.

It seems that for centuries no one has seen this mirror which is enclosed within many caskets. The oldest daughter of the emperor is traditionally the great priestess of Ise. She watches over the 400 holy articles which are kept there (including some magnificent swords) and which may not be filmed or photographed without her express permission, which is seldom granted.

The spiritual unity of Japan

The mystery and sense of the holy seem to envelop the Japanese people as a whole. The question, 'Where do the Japanese come from?' is often asked. It seems that from the earliest known prehistoric background of paleo-Siberian origin, various populations from Southern China and possibly Melanesia merged together. In the 3rd century BC numerous families from south of the Yangtzekiang settled in the north of Kyushu bringing with them the use of iron and bronze and the culture of rice. In the 3rd century AD bands of archers on horseback came from Altai via Korea, established themselves as masters on the islands and formed the framework of the future Japanese nation as an identifiable unity.

This unity of Japan, of which Mount Fuji is a symbol, itself deserves reflection. It is totally false in one sense and totally natural in another. Natural because it is made up of people living on relatively small islands, separated from the mainland; false in the sense that it occurred quite late. In fact, in the very beginning, because of the geographical relief of Japan with its enclosed valleys sometimes separated by very high mountains and with its widely dispersed islands displaying very different climates, primitive Japan was peopled with ethnic groups each very different from the others with few common characteristics, possibly not even a common language.

Today, the kanushi or priests of the Shinto temples are served by young virgins or miko. Here, a miko dressed in white and red is ringing bells in honour of the kami.

What caused them to be united? First of all, it was the feeling of belonging to one land as opposed to a continent which had many different collections of customs.

This national consciousness took place rather late if one considers that the great Chinese Empire had already attained a high degree of civilization at a time when Japan was still peopled with tribes.

During the good and the bad times in its history, the unity of Japan, personified in the emperor, embodies above all a principle of immanence. Although often mocked and reduced to a caricature personified by these very same emperors, this principle has protected Japan to this day. In the face of transience and the vacuity of everything, the Japanese have throughout the centuries chosen continuity, or the system of ancestors, families, masters and traditions.

Whatever the deficiencies of this system,

unity and continuity have managed to survive throughout the turmoils of history. The emperor is no longer worshipped officially as a god, nevertheless he is one, being the first Shinto priest and his real power remains the only fundamental power giving Japan its identity which reaches beyond his own image. If such a power were to disappear, it is likely that the centuries-old Japan that we know today would at once cease to exist.

This sense of permanence, loosely linked to the impermanence of the Japanese soul, does not communicate itself easily. A life is worth nothing if it is not the expression of a destiny which prolongs it as a mirror reflects the true image. Death is worth nothing if it does not face a destiny which is in the end richer than life itself. Hence, the contempt of death and the sense of self-sacrifice which are inherent in the Japanese soul.

A Shinto ceremony on a holy hill (utaki) on the island of Okinawa. Although the ceremony is conducted by a Shinto priest (kanushi), the old women-priests (noro) still play an important role. The harai-gushi which the priest shakes from side to side ensures purification both for the gods and the people. (The harai-gushi is made from strips of paper cut up and attached to the end of a stick.)

The practice of Shinto

The Shinto prayer or norito is primarily an invocation and consists of naming the kami. Nothing is asked of the gods as they know the needs of mankind. Said the sage Miyamoto Musashi, one of the greatest masters of the sword in Japan: one must worship the gods and gain their esteem but never ask any favours. Clapping hands and bowing is a way of calling upon the kami and of praying. After the norito and offerings to the kami: sake (or rice wine), water, salt, fish, fruit and vegetables, and once the prayers are over, the priest shakes a harai-gushi made from strips of paper cut up and attached to the end of a stick. This is the sign of the purification for men and gods alike.

Many of these festivals involve purification rites. Arrows are sold in a temple, then taken home where they are charged with all the impurities and at the end of the year burnt at a religious ceremony. Sometimes it is the miko, Shinto priestesses, who cleanse the arrows brought by the faithful, with their dancing, or else one draws or writes down whatever one wishes to be rid of on pieces of white paper. These bits of paper are taken to the sanctuary and thrown into a river by the priests.

At one time it was the practice to confide one's secrets to the great ears of a horse. This is why Shinto still reveres the horse today.

When the kami are present, the priestess sings and dances, representing the union of heaven and earth. (Dance of a noro in the Futenmangu cave near Naha, Okinawa.)

Shinto temples are places where the kami are worshipped. The shimenawa, enormous plaited ropes found above the entrance of many temples, signify a place which is both holy and purified.

One cannot enter the heart of a Shinto sanctuary until hands and mouth have been purified with water from a fountain. Similarly, the practice employed by many Shinto sects of immersing the whole body in the sea at the beginning of the year has its origins in the myth of the god Izanagi who cleansed his body in the sea on his return from the underworld. These purification rites are held on the occasion of a birth or a death, for in Shinto death creates impurity. That is why the practice of entombing the dead is confined to the Buddhist religion. Shinto is only interested in life and all its ages. Life on earth is therefore a happy event, a satisfaction which the divine spirit requires.

Up until now, Shinto and Buddhism have come a long way together in Japan. Both religions, having influenced each other throughout the centuries to the point of forming various syncretic schools, including Ryobu Shinto (a mixture of Shinto and Buddhism), have since the accession of Emperor Meiji 100 years ago regained their integrity. The future of these two religions is proving to be identical, for the vitality of Shinto lies in being so close to nature that it can only survive on equal terms, immutable in spite of the violations to which nature is nowadays subjected, together with all that is delicate and immensely vital which is part of nature.

The Japan of the samurai

THE WAY OF THE WARRIOR OR BUSHIDO

The spirit of Bushido or law of the Samurai

This is concerned essentially with the Way of the sword rather than sword fighting. A man who only learns sword techniques cannot hope to survive for long, even less to achieve true mastership. Bushido imposes rules such that man ceases to concentrate on the use of the sword and, in its image, learns how to become pure, serene and immutable.

The rigid rules of bushido influence every minute of the life of a true samurai. These same rules, later codified, are countless and cover every aspect of behaviour both internal and external. In actual fact, bushido, the origin of which dates from before the founding of the Kamakura Shogunate (1192), with the warlike precepts of the Minamoto clan, had considerable influence on the spirit and customs of the Japanese.

The meaning of bushido

The word bushido has been popularized by Nitobe in his work *Bushido, Soul of Japan,* written in 1899. Since then it is accepted that the word should embrace the many warlike rules governing samurai life and art of war. The word is made up of the contraction of *bushi* meaning warrior and *do*, the Way or moral. Bushido therefore means the Way of the warrior.

The three ages of bushido are:

1. Ancient martial bushido or kyuba no michi (Way of the bow and the horse). This had its origins in the onset of rivalry between the Taira and Minamoto clans around the 11th century and it continued until the end of the internal wars.

Horseman with bow.

The rule of the 'bow and the horse' came into use as a samurai code of conduct during the Kamakura period (13th century). In return for the honour of being a samurai and of having the right to the bow and the horse, the duties were severe and numerous.

The other warriors or bushi were ordinary people (Kootsunin or Bonge).

The samurai of Japan, who ceased to exist less than a century ago, knew how to impart their science of combat and their training. Today, Japan perpetuates their memory by holding many festivals and processions. The generals alone had the right to wear a crescent on their helmets. The armour dates from the 17th century and is strictly authentic.
Portrayal of samurai and ronin going into battle.

2. Reformed bushido. An amalgamation of Confucianism, Shinto and Buddhism which emerged with the founding of the Tokugawa Shogunate (1603) and was only codified under the name bushido at the beginning of the 17th century.

3. Modern bushido, since the restoration of the imperial regime at the beginning of the Meiji era (1868).

The Way of the bow and the horse

The Way of the bow and the horse (kyuba no michi) was the very first unwritten law of the samurai at the end of the 12th century. It is much more accurate to use the word 'Way' rather than 'law'. Traditionally, the Way is

what absorbs man's whole being. The law is a judicial system which one obeys either voluntarily or under constraint. The Way, moreover, gives the idea of a constant but unending attempt at one's own perfection; the law by its nature is determined and defined once and for all.

In fact, as Pierre Landy says of bushido, 'it is the product, named much later, of a long heritage of Shinto, Buddhist, Confucian, national and Chinese precepts, or derivations of the strict customs of a rural population. In it one finds ancestor worship, obedience to the sovereign, probity of heart and spirit, patience, resignation to the inevitable, contempt of death.'[1]

Bushido, in spite of all other influences, is an expression of the pure but strong Japanese character.

[1] *Japan,* published (in French) by Nagel, p.242.

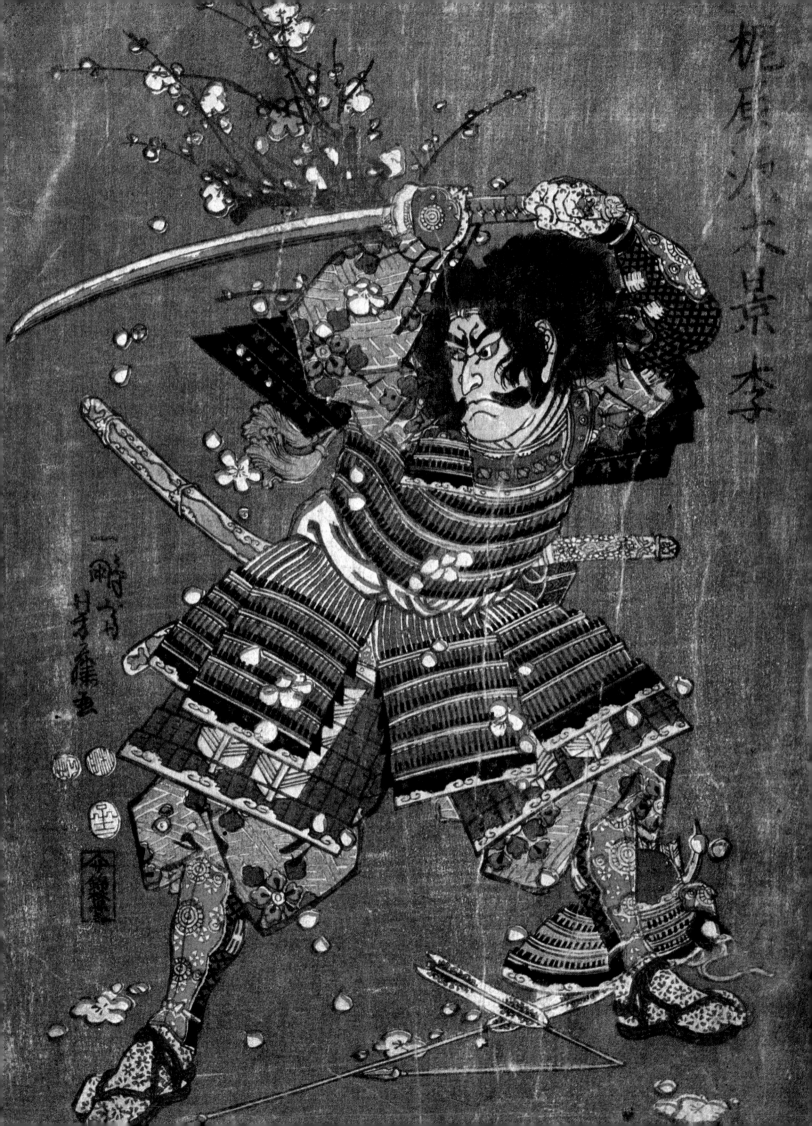

The giri notion and moral duty

Bushido philosophy, usually interpreted as 'samurai law', has certainly simplified for the benefit of the West a notion which is very much more subtle, concerning not only the samurai law of life or of honour, but also a code of existence which has always been in itself unique to the Japanese people and which can be summarized by the giri notion, loosely translated by the words 'duty', 'uprightness', or 'rectitude' (which is essential for personal honour). Each class of the population therefore has a particular giri and the higher one climbs in society, the more demanding this duty becomes. It is therefore understandable that as the samurai were considered to be the uppermost class in Japan, the giri or code of ethics which they followed encompassed the most rigorous demands of all the social hierarchy.

Through the centuries, many books have expounded in minute detail the qualities inherent in the Way of the warrior. The best known are the *Budo Shoshin Shu* or *Elementary Readings on Bushido*, written by an erudite samurai, Daidoji Yuzan (1639-1730) and the *Buke Sho Hatto* written at the request of the shogun Tokogawa Ieyasu and his successor, in order to set down the respective rules of conduct of the *bushi* or *buke* (warriors) and the noblemen of the court. The *Koyo Gunkan* (early 17th century) is made up of 20 volumes and attributed to Kosaka Danjo Nobumasa, himself an associate of Obata Kagenori (1572-1662) who used his name. The work proposes as a model Takedu Shingen, the great samurai and lord of the province of Kaishu which never suffered defeat. 'Every battle started must be won' is the guiding principle of the *Gunkan*.

Momonari helmet, about 1700.

Armour of the Edo period.

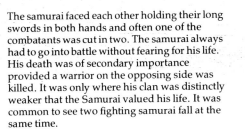

The samurai faced each other holding their long swords in both hands and often one of the combatants was cut in two. The samurai always had to go into battle without fearing for his life. His death was of secondary importance provided a warrior on the opposing side was killed. It was only where his clan was distinctly weaker that the Samurai valued his life. It was common to see two fighting samurai fall at the same time.

A warrior at the time of Kamakura. Print by Ichieisai Yoshifuji (Edo period).

Armour from the middle of the Edo period.

Oshi Eboshi type helmet worn by the Maeda, Kaga Province.

The Concept of death or the Hagakure law

In 1716, the 11 volumes of *Hagakure* were completed (the word means 'hidden beneath the leaves' and it was to become one of the most famous works extolling bushido in Japan). the author, Yamamoto Tsunetomo, was a monk and former samurai of the Saga clan on Kyushu.

He wrote the book after the death of his master whom he survived by ten years, preferring the monastic life of deprivation and meditation to committing suicide as many vassals tended to do on the death of their lord. That is why the thought of death forms the main theme of the book and, in particular, the following passage which has made the work famous in Japan:

'I realized that bushido signified death. When one is forced to choose between life and death, the important thing is to be able to make the choice without hesitation, without weighing up the pros and cons in endless meditation. One should be able to decide quite simply and act. The idea that it is pointless to die without attaining one's aims in life is frivolous and despicable, characteristic of the people from Kyoto and Osaka. It is an undeniable fact that we all prefer life to death, which is why there are so many people who like to think that the course we like best is the right one. In fact, he who cannot continue to live while witnessing the failure of his ambitions is a coward. It is vain to think that one cannot die leaving behind unfulfilled objectives. It is a fallacy – it is not dishonourable. It is there and there alone that the true spirit of bushido emerges. If a samurai practises introspection and self-criticism all the time and if, in addition, he is disposed to give his life where and when the need arises, he will be perfect in all the martial arts and lead an exemplary life.'

The work concludes that, of the two options, life or death, it is always far better to choose death. Given the choice of avowed love or secret love, it is better to remain silent and keep the love secret. This notion of death introduces a complete theme which must nevertheless comprise appreciable nuances.

Suhara, the master, one of the principals of the Zen temple at Engakuji, in meditation. He is also a great master of kyujutsu/kyudo.

The coats of arms or mon have at all times played an important role in Japan. (*double spread overleaf*).

The relationship of life to death

In Shinto, life has been seen to be a gift of the gods. Therefore, one must not risk one's life pointlessly and a samurai who trifled with his existence or that of others was discredited. There again, the giri notion intervenes. As long as the natural order portrays universal internal harmony, life is worth living. If this order is seriously upset, it is better to die than to live.

The true spirit of the Way, frequently expressed by the great masters, can be summarized as follows: it is fitting always to protect life as long as life is appropriate. It is by understanding the detachment of death that one can appreciate the value of life. On the other hand, the fixed idea which causes man to overcome fear of death and the way in which the delicate flower of the cherry tree is symbolic of life's impermanence, is a method of reducing the totality of existence to a form of fulfilment of life.

Of course, these qualities involve other internal attitudes such as the desire for non-possession, or at least complete detachment with regard to worldly goods. The very idea of acquiring contempt of death is doubtless easy to express but how much more difficult to put it into practice! In other words, a man who has actually achieved detachment from death is undoubtedly liberated as he has nothing more to learn.

The right attitude in the face of death

The whole question is therefore to imagine what one's attitude should be when faced with death: 'To hurl oneself into the thick of the battle and get killed is relatively easy' said a lord from Mito. It is quite easy and within the reach of the most simple-minded churl, but the essence of true courage lies in knowing when to live and to die only when death is necessary.

Seppuku or ritual suicide

It is difficult to write about the Way of the sword without introducing at least one of the customs for which Japan is noted throughout the world and which reveals the Japanese in a

The foot soldiers and samurai who had no master became ronin. A ronin often lived by teaching the martial arts. In times of war, if he did not own a horse, he had to fight in the infantry. If he became a flag bearer, he was entitled to a bamboo spear.

The samurai constituted the uppermost class in Japan. It is thought that between 1603 and 1867 they numbered between 450,000 and 500,000 in Japan.

The samurai were part of the bushi or warrior class, hence the name of the samurai code of conduct: bushido (do meaning the Way, bu being the warrior and shi the family or clan). Bushido is understood to be the way of obedience to the master.

Samurai flag bearer.

Hara-kiri or ritual suicide beneath flowering cherry trees symbolic of the beauty and transience of life. Hara-kiri or seppuku was carried out with a small sword or wakizashi. A devoted friend prepares to cut off his head. Illustration by Toyokouni.

particular light: the seppuku rite or, in more usual terms, hara-kiri or ritual suicide by disembowelment. It is hard to find a more delicate subject than hara-kiri in Japan, for what may at first sight appear to be a well-established, acceptable Japanese institution, motivated by the apparently traditional spirit of bushido, is in fact clothed in ambiguity, in spite of the outward simplicity of the concept, so that it is necessary to cover a little of the history in order to relate it accurately to this Japanese tradition.

In the first place, as has already been said, Japan was essentially moved by the Shinto spirit, even before its time. (That is, before Shinto was given its name in the 6th century with the advent of Buddhism.) According to ancient Japanese belief, death is a despicable event. Throughout the centuries, to this day, it is remarkable that Seppuku has never taken place, for example, in the setting of a Shinto temple, for the act demands that the Shinto priest who officiates (rarely) at the death rite should afterwards undertake at least three days of purification and the extraordinary complexity of these ceremonies discourages the practice of funeral rites within the framework of the Shinto religion.

In later centuries, when a bridge, castle, or any other building was being constructed which required the protection of the gods, it was sometimes customary to sacrifice one or several consenting people who thus became kami protectors of the building and were called 'human pillars' (hito-bashira). This custom was prohibited at the end of the 17th century.

With the advent of the samurai caste system, the idea arose that nothing was more commendable for a vassal than to die once his master died. Buddhism accentuated the establishment of this custom of self-sacrifice as a sign of loyalty. The precariousness of human life, the transitory nature of the world and the acceptance of inevitable death, all these elements which according to the Buddhist point of view stemmed from unquestionable fatalism, contributed to the

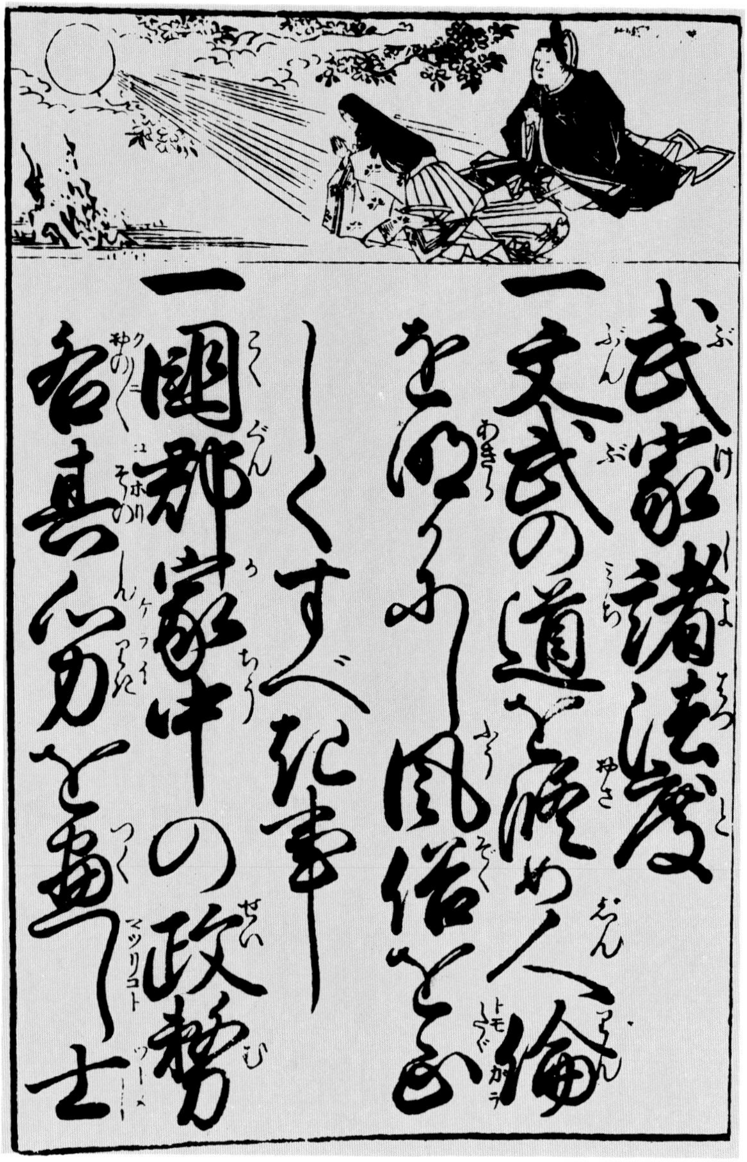

Opening page of the 'Buke Sho Hatto' or samurai code (Tokugawa era).

formation of the Samurai code of conduct. So, throughout the centuries, the practice of seppuku developed with the samurai, to the point where ritual suicide could be employed not only as a way of departing from life oneself but, on occasions, samurai who wished to reproach their master severely would sacrifice themselves at the door of his home as proof of their reprobation. It also followed that the death of a lord could give rise to a certain number of suicides.

Self-punishment and the personal acceptance of responsibility for an error is extremely common in Japan. That is why, when the country surrendered in 1945 and the emperor announced the end of the hostilities, many leading citizens committed hara-kiri before the moat of the imperial palace.

Nevertheless, although deep-rooted, this practice of suicide has only rarely been approved by the great masters. Many political or religious authorities tried alike to oppose it. In 1663, the feudal government or 'Bakufu' issued an edict in the following terms: 'We have on many occasions said that an inordinate act of suicide is both evil and futile. However, this view has never been officially defended until now. We have seen too many of our vassals commit suicide of late. Consequently, the edict forbids suicide and offenders' families will be stripped of their possessions or alternatively the blame will be laid on their children.' This did happen in the case of the families of one or two offenders who infringed the edict 25 years later. The two oldest sons were sentenced to hara-kiri, while the two daughters were banished.

In 1882, in support of the Bakufu edict, a prohibitive clause was added to the samurai penal code, putting an end to this custom. Since then, the infringement of the clause has always roused tremendous emotion in Japan, for example on the death of General Nogi and his wife on the occasion of the Emperor Meiji's funeral, or more recently the writer Mishima Yukio in 1972.

However, seppuku or suicide by decree as an instrument of justice has in a way remained a means by which the government or the emperor may punish or destroy a samurai without disrespect to the code of honour. In February 1868, some Japanese soldiers under the command of a samurai opened fire on foreigners arriving at the port of Kobe. Bisen, the samurai who was to blame, was sentenced to seppuku.

Bushido law in codified form

— True courage lies in living when it is right to live and dying when it is right to die.
— Think of death in the full knowledge of what the honour of a samurai demands (weighing up each word before speaking); ask yourself before replying whether what you have to say is true.
— Eat in moderation, avoiding indulgence.
— Remember the word 'death' when the daily chores are done; do not fail to keep it in mind.
— Respect the rule about the tree trunk and the branches. To forget it means never being able to understand what virtue is.
— A man who despises virtue is no samurai. The parents of every man represent the trunk of his own body whilst he is the kindred branch, the offspring of his parents.

— A samurai will behave as a son and faithful subject. He will not leave his overlord even if the number of his subjects is reduced from a hundred to ten or from ten to one.

— In time of war, as proof of his loyalty he will be required to go before the enemy arrows if necessary without fearing for his life.

— Loyalty, a spirit of justice and bravery are the three natural virtues of the samurai.

— A samurai, wherever he sleeps, must not point his legs in the direction of the home of his overlord. Similarly, when he practises bowmanship, he must not point or shoot his arrow in the direction of his overlord, neither when he lays down his spear.

— If he hears someone talking about his overlord, or if he himself speaks of him, he must, if he is lying down, stand up.

— The falcon will not eat the grain, even if he is starving. So a samurai who uses a toothpick will pretend he has feasted, even if he has eaten nothing.

— If in war a samurai loses the battle and is obliged to surrender his head, he will declare his name fearlessly when called upon to do so by the enemy and die smiling, not with a vile expression.

— If seriously wounded, so seriously that no surgical operation can cure him, he will speak correctly before his superiors and his equals and die composed, in the full realization of the state of his wound.

— A samurai whose only attribute is strength is not acceptable. He must use his leisure time to practise poetry and understand the tea ceremony, not to mention the necessity of science studies.

— A samurai may create a very sober tea room in his home provided he uses new kakemono, modern cups and an unvarnished teapot.

Taken from *Budo Shoshin Shu* by Daidoji Yuzan, 1639-1730.

The foot warriors (zusa) were usually barefoot or wore simple straw sandals. They were lightly armed, often with a spear or naginata and in war acted as aides or servants to the samurai. Some were allowed to carry bows and arrows.

During the Heian period (794-1192) some important changes took place at national level. A powerful family, the Fujiwara, tried to usurp the functions of Prime Minister and Regent by creating kinships with the imperial family.

So, as the power of the emperor declined, the safety of the Court itself, established at Heian Kyo (now called Kyoto) was precarious; hoards of bandits overran the country, threatening stately homes and the imperial palace at Kyoto. The leaders of the clans who owned land and property recruited peasants to protect their possessions, and this was the beginning of the samurai (from a word meaning 'to be at one's side'), a class of warriors in the service of noble families.

Two great rival families distinguished themselves, the Taira and the Minamoto. In the struggle which took place between them, Minamoto Yoritomo managed to destroy the Taira in the famous naval battle of Dan no Ura (1185) which has been the object of innumerable epic accounts in the course of history.

Yoshitsune, 19th-century portrait by Kuniyoshi.

In 1185, Yoshitsune won the famous battle of Dan no Ura against the Taira.

His half-brother, Yoritomo, jealous of his success and bravery, wanted to kill him. Yoshitsune fled and when he was on the point of being captured he killed himself according to the seppuku rite; his vassal then killed his master's wife and children before setting fire to the house and throwing himself into the flames (Ukiyoe, 1860).

HISTORICAL JAPAN AND THE ORIGIN OF THE SAMURAI

The ancient budo warrior: the Kamakura era (1192-1333)

The Kamakura era marks the introduction of warriors into the government. As yet, they only formed a minority, accustomed to a hard, even austere life, simply dressed and almost always on a war footing.

Yoritomo emerged as the leader in the reorganization of Japanese society. The rule of the bow and the horse (kyuba no michi) forbad any alliance or relationship with the aristocrats of the imperial court based in Heian-Kyo (Kyoto). Zen, recently intro-duced, reinforced the moral principles of the warriors. The samurai code of honour was imposed with its exacting ethics and rules which had to be strictly obeyed. However, with the rise of two new classes – warriors and merchants – Japan began to free herself from the single aristocratic class and prepare the way for the Japan of today.

Throughout the centuries, Yoshitsune's popularity has always been widespread (his image on a kite).

Burning of Sanjo Palace – third quarter of the 13th century. From a horizontal scroll, Boston Museum of Fine Arts. In the night of 9 December 1159,

Yoritomo, who was primarily a warrior, obviously knew how to turn the strict rules of feudal ethics to his advantage, forcing the vassals into absolute obedience and loyalty to their master. At the same time, the samurai constituted a privileged class in the country, a sort of knighthood, in that they rode horses and carried family emblems. On Yoritomo's death in 1199 at the age of 53, after falling from his horse, the samurai warriors had tight control over the country and even the noblemen at court.

Japan's history is the result of a fairly rare development of a nation which has never in the course of its history been conquered or enslaved by another until the arrival of MacArthur's forces. Japanese wars, however cruel and merciless, were always internal

wars between men and warriors with a common code of honour and combat, who faced death according to fixed rules, apparently accepted and recognized by both sides alike.

The Mongol invasion

Japan's only serious threat of invasion took place in the 13th century. On two occasions – in 1274 and 1281 – the Mongols, assisted by Koreans and Chinese, attacked and were repulsed.

During these attacks, the samurai were extremely surprised to discover that the Mongols did not fight according to the rules

Sanjo Palace was attacked and the former emperor, Goshirakawa, taken prisoner. The samurai are shown fighting desperately within the palace walls.

of honour they themselves practised. The first samurai who advanced before the invaders, declaring their names and defying the enemy according to custom, were simply massacred by arrows. The Japanese were no less surprised to find that the Mongols used techniques of fighting from a distance and their bows could fire short poisoned arrows about 200 yards, while they themselves were used to man-to-man combat. The Japanese long asymmetrical bows had at most a range of about 100 yards. Worse still, the Mongols who were masters in the art of scaring the enemy, used explosive devices and sounded enormous drums which terrified the horses.

Shortly after they first landed in 1274, the Mongols hastily reembarked, having lost about 13,500 men in a sudden storm,

according to Korean chronicles – the exact reason is not clear.

Warned by this first initiative, the Japanese reinforced their troops and built a stone wall 6ft 9in (2.10m) high and 8ft 11in (2.80m) thick along their coastlines. Vast reserves of men and arms were made ready. Seven years later, the largest invasion force in the memory of man appeared, as before, off Kyushu in the south of Japan. Two immense fleets, one carrying 50,000 men and the other 100,000 came into view. This time, the Japanese were prepared for anything.

The legendary terror which the very name of the Mongols, masters of the largest empire ever known, inspired had no effect on the Japanese. Scarcely had the Mongol ships been sighted when the Japanese, with their

51

characteristic contempt of death, rushed out to meet them in small boats in order to harrass and burn their ships.

The battle was confused and terrible and lasted 49 days. The Mongols used new and unfamiliar weapons, in particular bombs with fuses which on exploding threw the enemy into confusion and ballistas which hold great stone canon balls. The Mongols would have won in the end had it not been for a providential typhoon which destroyed the main part of their fleet in two days. Few men escaped the disaster and got away, for the Japanese beheaded a large number of prisoners. The providential typhoon was called *kamikaze* or holy wind.

In spite of the extreme danger they had just been through and the incontestable superiority of the Mongols in terms of weapons (bombs, stones, crossbows and powerful longbows), it is a remarkable fact that the Japanese retained with reverence their traditional weapons, including the sword (dreadful in man-to-man combat it is true) and the asymmetrical bow, which was only relatively effective. No one could have altered the samurai in their conviction that success in battle lay above all in man's skill with his weapon, rather than in the weapon itself.

This victory, dearly won, at the cost of many lives, did not eliminate the danger and, until about 1320, the shogunate kept troops in readiness for war along the whole length of the coastline. When Kublai Khan died however in 1294, the Mongols abandoned their quest for adventure in Japan. But something occurred which ended feudalism in Japan: all the warriors who had been kept in arms for years demanded compensation. Usually, in struggles between clans, the conqueror would help himself to booty from the conquered. On this occasion, however, there was nothing to share out; the shogunate did its best to try and distribute some lands amongst the samurai who had fought best but of course it could not distribute more in the way of riches than it possessed. There was very little to go round as the country had been bled dry. This caused growing discontent amongst the samurai who felt wronged.

Mongol archer.

52

Said to be a portrait of Taira No Shigemori (1138-79), the oldest son of Taira no Kiyomori who seized power at the end of the 12th century. He is seen here in ceremonial dress, sitting on a mat and holding his badge of rank. Attributed to Fujiwara Takenobu (1142-1205) from a silk scroll kept at the Jingoji, Kyoto.

Hideyoshi, here still in the service of his Master Nobunaga, crossing a ford in a river.

The Muromachi era (1336-1574): the three great dictators

This situation was to lead to a progressive state of anarchy in Japan. Although temporarily restored, the imperial authority was to be challenged by the Ashikaga clan.

For 50 years, up until 1392, Japan had two emperors: one in the north, appointed by the shogun; the other, in the south, considered itself lawful. Unity seemed to revive in 1392 but the shogunate, by this time weak and decadent, could not prevent bloody battles for superiority between families and clans. The city of Kyoto itself was even destroyed.

From 1574, three great dictators emerged: Oda Nobunaga (1573-82), Hideyoshi (1582-98), and Tokugawa Ieyasu (1600-56). Paradoxically, all three came from modest backgrounds, which was in itself a revolution in terms of Japanese history, for until then all the leaders had come from the nobility. With them came the age of the dictator generals and it is they who unified Japan for the very first time.

For the next 25 or 30 years, Japan was to witness a new era. All the clans which hitherto had made war on each other had to obey and submit to the central authority.

Hideyoshi, in distributing fiefs to his army officers, took care as a skilful politician to make them masters of provinces distant from their families in order to exercise better control over them. Then he ordered a census of all the lands and fixed the amount of taxes which every farmer should pay. This census embarrassed many land owning peasants who, during the recent wars had managed to conceal the true size of their properties in order to avoid taxes. But Hideyoshi intensified his efforts and severely suppressed all revolts, so as to permit an accurate census of all the land belonging either to the peasants, the great landowners, or the monasteries, thus gaining real power over the peasants. This system made them virtually independent but it also tied them to their land, compelling them to farm it in order to pay the taxes which had been imposed according to the surface area and type of soil of their estate. This census took a long time and sometimes Hideyoshi was obliged to take radical steps in order to enforce the law on the peasants. In 1588, they were forbidden to possess weapons and these either had to be converted into instruments of culture or handed over to government agents.

'. . . If the people only possess tools of culture and devote themselves exclusively to agriculture, they and their descendants will prosper. The good of the people is the object of this order which is fundamental to the peace and security of the country and the happiness of the people . . .' (extract from *Kokushi Gaikan* by Kuroita, dated Tensho 16, 7th month, 8th day). In 1591, Hideyoshi gave strict orders for keeping the peasants on their own land, thus creating the basis of a rigid social order which, under the Tokugawa and at the cost of semi-enslavement of the rural classes, kept the peace and established the principle of collective responsibility: 'If a peasant forsakes his fields, either to go into business or to become a merchant or worker, he must be punished and his whole village prosecuted with him. All those who are not employed in military service or engaged in farming the land are to be questioned by the local authorities and expelled . . . In cases concerning the disappearance of peasants who have deserted their land to go into business, the whole town or village is to be held responsible for the offence . . . No soldier who has left his master without permission may be taken on by another. If this rule is infringed and the soldier has been allowed to go, three men must be offered as compensation to the first master . . .' (extract from *Kokushi Shiryo Shu III*, dated Tensho 19,

8th month, 21st day). In other instances, Hideyoshi threatened to put to death, together with their entire family, those peasants who opposed the inspectors and to destroy any village which showed signs of insubordination. The peasants had to pay in tax a lump sum equivalent to 40 or 50 per cent of the value of their harvest. They had just enough left to keep them from starvation.[1]

As for the lords, their conditions were none the more enviable, considering their position. Every action was governed by tyrannical rules: they could not leave the court at Kyoto unless they left their family behind as hostages and their troops were limited to 20 armed men.

Under financial pressure and at the mercy of the power of absolute despotism, whatever class they belonged to, the Japanese could do nothing but resign themselves. Furthermore, a spy network kept Japan under the surveillance of the shogun.

Reformed bushido

Reformed bushido (a mixture of Confucianism and Zen) first appears at the beginning of the Tokugawa shogunate (1603).

The government of the time, covering a period of 264 years, is distinguished by the fact that it was in every respect a samurai government. This was the Edo era (1603-1868). The supreme military commanders governed the feudal lords with absolute power over people and property. The samurai and the warriors constituted the top social class; they had the power of life and death over any man of a lower class. After them came the peasants, the workers and finally the merchants.

However, the Tokugawa era was also a peaceful time. There were no more internal wars and the samurai had no cause to exercise their swords. Many became farmers, others ronin (out of work samurai) but the majority became military officials.

[1] Louis Frédéric: *Japan, art and civilisation*, AMG, Paris, 1969.

Samurai with gun.

The first fire arms appeared in Japan in 1543 and a number of Samurai considered themselves obliged to use them (until the arrival of Commodore Perry, the only fire arms in use were primitive matchlocks). But most of the time they preferred to confront their enemies in the open and to fight with the sword. (Print attributed to Iku Yoshi.)

Ancient bushido was no longer relevant to modern times. The famous Zen priest, Takuan (1573-1645), explained bushido from the Zen point of view; many authors have given a Confucianist version of it.

The proliferation of writings concerning the samurai discipline of life no doubt stemmed from the dangerous idleness in which they found themselves. Although fire arms were henceforth generally manufactured in Japan, the true samurai adopted a supreme contempt of them, extolling the virtues of their two swords which they agreed to demonstrate from then on in the form of stylish displays.

The author of the *Budo Shoshin Shu,* written at the beginning of the 17th century, does not fail to point out the extent to which things had changed:

'At the time of the internal wars, a samurai reached adulthood at the age of 15 or 16. His training or handling of weapons began at the age of 12 or 13, so he hardly had time to sit at a desk. It was therefore a time when many samurai could neither read nor write.

'Nevertheless, one could not accuse them of laziness, nor reproach their parents for having neglected their education: it was just that exercises in the handling of weapons were by far the most important thing as far as they were concerned.'

The Tokugawa era also saw Japan close her doors (from 1639). Christians who had at first been tolerated (Jesuits in particular), were gradually harried and later persecuted. For two centuries, Japan under shogun rule gave free rein to an anti-Western xenophobia. The English, French, Americans, Portuguese, Spanish, Russians, all of whom tried to establish commercial relationships with Japan, came up against unrelenting ostracism.

In 1854, Commodore Perry, leading a powerful squadron, forced the shogunate to sign a treaty of friendship with the United States. This treaty was also ratified with most of the other Western nations, thus ending a long period of isolation.

Suddenly Japan became aware that having remained independent of Western progress for two centuries, the country had become extremely vulnerable. The signing of the treaties had been imposed and was regarded as a great defeat. The superiority of Western arms was the country's greatest fear.

A dramatic change was taking place in the soul of Japan: without arms or allies she would have to swallow her immense pride on

The fifteenth and last shogun, Yoshinobu Tokugawa, declares his renunciation of power on 7 November 1867 at Nijo Castle in Kyoto.

two counts: in the face of the brute force imposed by the treaties, and in the eyes of the detested civilization of the barbarians to whose school of thought they were forced to submit. The speed with which Japan abolished the old regime was a measure of her concern. In 1867, the fifteenth shogun, Tokugawa Keiki, restored political power to the emperor. Thus ended the power of the samurai, first established at the end of the 13th century.

For six centuries, the samurai caste system had represented the basis of the whole feudal establishment. It is true that during periods of peace the samurai lost their sense of direction and their life became difficult, which sometimes caused them to revolt against the shogun government in spite of themselves.

But of course their political influence was still considerable and to some extent fostered feudal rivalries, the cause of civil war. It is thought that between 1603 and 1867 the number of samurai fluctuated between 450,000 and 500,000.

Portrait of Emperor Meiji.

Japan was passing from a nation of craftsmen into the industrial age. The industrialization of Japan during the seventies was not brought about by economic necessity nor social reality. It was considered essential to Japan's political independence. For better or worse, the majority of samurai accepted this new life. Former samurai even went so far as to send their daughters (sons less frequently) out to work in factories.

Social classes having been suppressed, conscription was introduced, but the old bushi (warriors) did not conceal their scorn for the rabble whom they were to command. In effect, all sorts of individuals became soldiers. In spite of reservations and difficulties, the new army began to take shape. Only the authority of the emperor could, as a last resort, force the samurai into submission.

Nevertheless, Saigo Takamori – a samurai who had assisted in the restoration of the empire – revolted. He managed to form an army of 42,000. The government, for its part, mobilized more than 60,000 men, pursued Saigo and decimated at least half his army. In spite of Saigo's defeat, however, the Japanese militarists continued to exercise considerable influence.

The end of the samurai

The year 1868 marks the end of the shogun in Japan, that is to say the end of military hegemony and a return to the power of the emperors. Emperor Meiji introduced a new constitution and opened his country to the West. At the same time, the samurai lost all their privileges. In 1870, Emperor Meiji, by formally abolishing feudalism, apparently rang the death knell of bushido. Two years later, the samurai gave up their traditional hairstyle, which involved keeping the front part of the head completely shaved and the hair at the back gathered on the neck and tied on the crown of the head.

In 1876, it was forbidden to carry a sword and its teaching was prohibited; those who did not comply were imprisoned. For a while, the samurai who resisted the wind of change in history were poor and persecuted.

Modern bushido

In spite of the disappearance of the samurai and of feudal practices, traditional Japan remained alive.

Modern Japan demonstrated during the last war – even beyond the famous exploits of the Kamikaze – that the old rules which, for example, forbade a warrior to surrender, were still effective. The identity of the nation as a whole, personified in the emperor, and its unconditional submission to his decisions are all part of the same spirit.

The principles of bushido still play an important role in big business. When all is said and done, economic competition conforms to a strategy laid down by a small group of men who put the interests of the Great Japan before private interests.

Emperor Meiji with his leading dignitaries listening to the reading of the imperial order which was the birth of modern-day Japan, 6 April 1868.

The unwritten law in Japan

So, bushido emerges as the unwritten law of the Japanese. The Japanese mentality is so strongly imbued with it that it is hard to imagine things changing. Their society is based on an idea of bondage and interdependence. The group comes before the individual. The relationship is one of overlord to vassal. Within the family, the children's dependence on their parents is still very strong. The spread of Buddhism and Confucianism and the very basis of the Shinto spirit lend strength to this state of affairs. At the top, 3000 or 4000 people in the fields of politics, culture, religion and economy still govern the 100 million Japanese. This omnipresent hierarchy is the key to Japan.

Japanese military policy and the Great Japan (1937-45)

After the Saigo Takamori revolt had been crushed in 1877, a strange man emerged: Toyama Mitsuru, aged 23. Toyama wanted a strong pure nation. He dreamt of a Japan, faithful to its traditions, to the kami, and faithful to the reverence of the emperor, a living god. He rejected an imperial regime which was becoming constitutional. As much a conspirator as an ascetic, Toyama Mitsuru wanted to avenge the death of Saigo Takamori. Shortly after, Okubo Toshimichi, Minister of the Interior, was assassinated. After that, the 'pure Japanese spirit' became dominant.

Military clans gained control. On 1 August

Japan's first overseas mission headed by Prince Iwa Kura, Ambassador Extraordinary and Plenipotentiary, leaving Yokohama for the United States and Europe, 23 December 1871.

1894, Japan declared war on China. A brief victorious campaign led the Japanese to the gates of Peking. They landed in Korea, took Port Arthur, and pushed forward into Manchuria.

But the Japanese had to give up Port Arthur when Russian troops moved in. Toyama Mitsuru then inspired the founding of a vast secret society called The Black Dragon which spread from Turkestan to Manchuria. Its pledge was to expel all whites from the Asian world. Within a few years, many moderate individuals had in turn been assassinated.

The authors of these 'patriotic' crimes were greatly admired. The courts only imposed nominal sentences. The conspirators likewise liquidated all the leading members of the government and submitted their demands to His Imperial Majesty:

— That the disloyal advisors be expelled
— That all political parties be dissolved
— Finally that the extreme nationalist general, Sadao Araki, be appointed commander in chief of the Manchurian army.

Modern Japan's greatest military rebellion had a grim ending. The emperor repudiated the rebels and they were all executed. After that, members of the nationalist military coalition were to occupy the key posts in the government. The military dictators who were installed considered themselves powerful enough to face the world. They were not afraid of China in its vastness, nor of the United States. For eight years (1937-45) they tried to involve every Japanese citizen in the myth of the Great Japan.

The Dai Nihon – Great Japan – is the period in which the nationalist leaders believed in Japanese supremacy over the whole of eastern Asia and the South Seas.

Japan 1945

At the beginning of 1945, however, Japan was in a very serious position. The defensive line in the Pacific had been overcome, the blockade and the bombings proved without question that the enemy was still advancing towards the metropolitan area.

In spite of the lassitude of the population and scepticism of some politicians, the armed forces still declared their faith in victory and, during the summer of 1945, they feverishly prepared to defend their national sanctuary and to crush the enemy in a last desperate effort, as soon as he set foot on their native soil.

The explosion of the two atomic bombs dropped on Hiroshima and Nagasaki on 6 and 9 August 1945, combined with Russia's intervention in the war by invading Manchuria, provoked extraordinary agitation within the Japanese cabinet. Lengthy discussions took place to decide whether or not the war should be continued. Finally, the only question left unsolved was that of safeguarding and protecting the imperial institutions. The advocates of peace won in the end, the conclusion being that a rapid end to the hostilities would in itself help to preserve these institutions.

For the first time in Japan's history, the emperor himself – Hirohito – addressed the nation. On 15 August 1945, he read out a message over the radio, veiled in such archaic and obscure terms that it took several hours for the country as a whole to realize that the emperor had agreed to capitulate unconditionally.

In the end, it was Japan's total cohesion with the emperor which once again saved the country from disruption. The United States were in effect obliged to recognize the emperor as the one valid spokesman in the construction of a new Japan, quite different to the one which had just collapsed.

In front of the skeleton of the Hall of Industry on Hiroshima, preserved as a reminder of the first atomic bomb, children represent Japan's rebirth and her future.

In those days, it was customary in Japan to give presents to officials whose service was requested. Asano subscribed to this practice and his presents were a measure of the service expected. However, Kira was an extremely corruptible official. Rankled by the fact that the gifts he received were not proportionate to Asano's considerable wealth, he decided not to help him but did not tell him so.

Asano managed as best he could. When the shogun gave an official reception to bid the imperial envoys farewell, Asano should have been in the front line but as he did not know exactly where he ought to be, nor what he should do, he asked the advice of Kira who replied:

The execution of Kira by Asano; print by Hiroshige.

Samurai preparing for battle.

STORY OF THE 47 RONIN

In the year 1701, the shogun Tokugawa Tsunayoshi had to receive in his castle three ambassadors from Emperor Higashiyama, who had come to present the emperor's New Year greetings, as was the custom.

The shogun organized a grand reception for them and appointed a great lord or 'Daimyo' from Ako Castle master of ceremonies. The lord, Asano Naganori, not being familiar with court customs, declined the honour and only accepted in the end on the express condition that the great master of ceremonies of the time, an old man named Kira Yoshihisa, assisted him.

'You should have thought of that before; I have not time to explain now.' And Kira went away with a very insulting remark.' Livid with rage, Asano drew his sword and wounded the old man in the face.

When Kira was taken away, the shogun heard what had happened and was extremely angry. He had Asano arrested and sentenced him to commit suicide by disembowelment two days later.

Asano wrote his farewell poem recalling his 36 years, scattered like petals, and then without hesitation disembowelled himself according to the rules of seppuku, after which an assistant cut off his head.

All his possessions were confiscated and overnight the 300 warriors who served Ako Castle found themselves out of work, in other words ronin.

They dispersed, but one – Oishi Kuranosuke – could not accept what had happened. He reunited 47 samurai and between them they decided to avenge their master. But the task was not an easy one as Kira suspected possible vengeance and had their every move and action watched. So, Oishi and his friends decided to give a false impression. They led a dissipated life, getting drunk and frequenting the geisha, by all appearances seeming even to have forgotten their master's memory.

Eventually the surveillance ceased and one snowy December night in the year 1702, they attacked Kira's home. He fled and hid whilst his warriors put up a brave fight. When found, he was decapitated and with his head wrapped in a white cloth, the samurai went to the Sengakuji temple where their master was entombed. There, they solemnly laid Kira's head, together with the dagger which had cut it off, and a note claiming responsibility for their action.

When they gave themselves up, the people of Edo greeted them as heroes and the shogun himself admired their courage and perseverance. But the law was the law. After several months' deliberation, the 47 ronin were ordered to commit ritual suicide which they did on 4 February 1703.

Their tombs were dug alongside that of their master, Asano. One of them, whom Oishi had sent to inform Asano's family that their master had been avenged, did not kill himself. He was acquitted on the grounds that the trial was closed, and he lived to be 83. Even so, on his death, his tomb was put alongside that of his friends.

These tombs are still much revered in Japan. Sticks of incense burn day and night on the tombstones. The story itself has been told thousands of times in every possible way and the Japanese still find it very moving.

Asano's faithful followers, arrested on the Bridge of Rioogokou by a government official (facsimile of a Japanese drawing).

JAPANESE ARMOUR

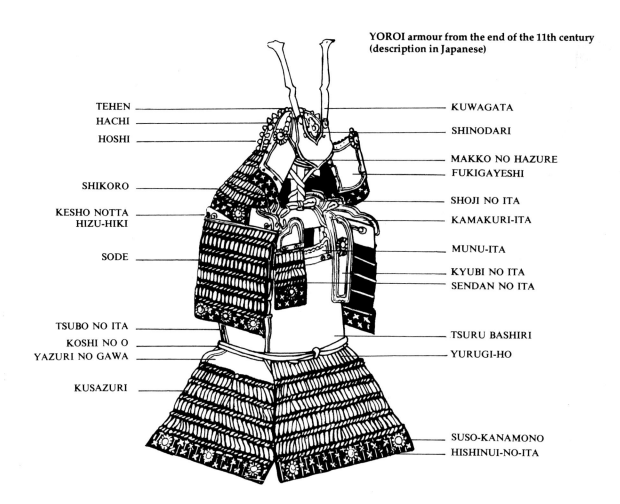

YOROI armour from the end of the 11th century
(description in Japanese)

KUWAGATA
SHINODARI
MAKKO NO HAZURE
FUKIGAYESHI
SHOJI NO ITA
KAMAKURI-ITA
MUNU-ITA
KYUBI NO ITA
SENDAN NO ITA
TSURU BASHIRI
YURUGI-HO
SUSO-KANAMONO
HISHINUI-NO-ITA

TEHEN
HACHI
HOSHI
SHIKORO
KESHO NOTTA
HIZU-HIKI
SODE
TSUBO NO ITA
KOSHI NO O
YAZURI NO GAWA
KUSAZURI

KABUTO helmets

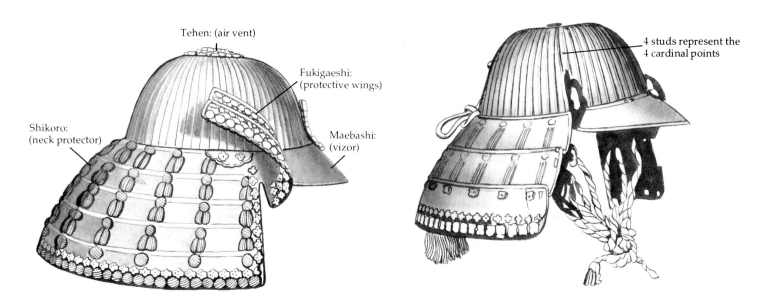

Tehen: (air vent)

Fukigaeshi:
(protective wings)

Shikoro:
(neck protector)

Maebashi:
(vizor)

4 studs represent the
4 cardinal points

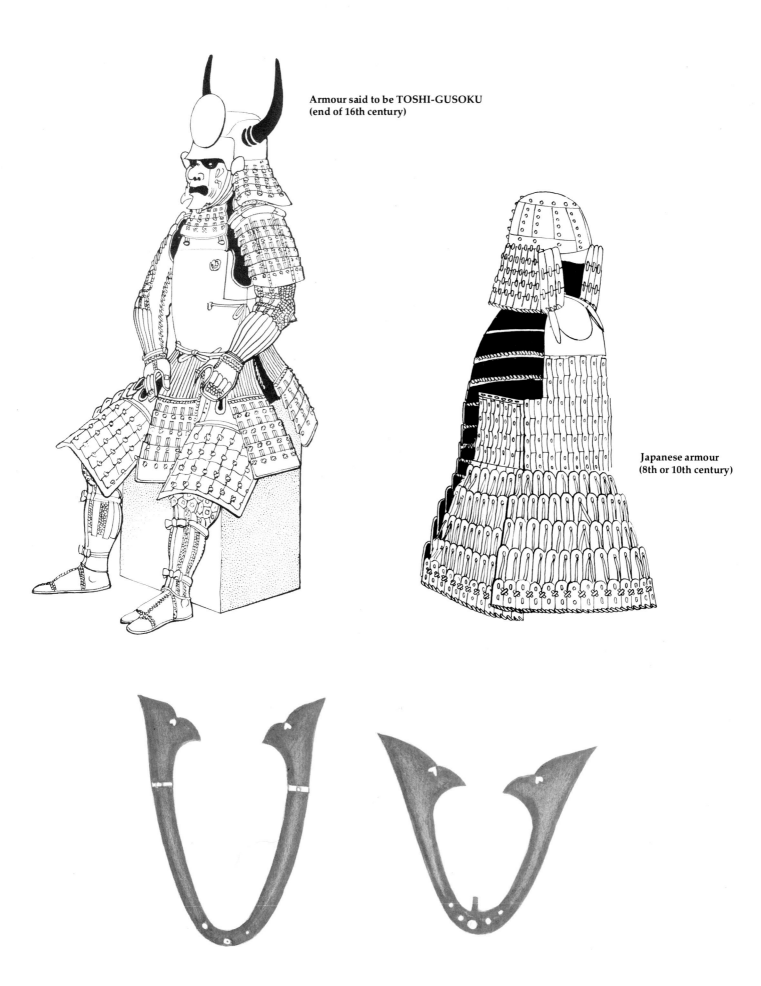

Armour said to be TOSHI-GUSOKU
(end of 16th century)

Japanese armour
(8th or 10th century)

MAEDATE frontal decorations

The three great Ways or

the spirit of budo

The spirit of budo

The spirit of the martial arts is no different to that of traditional budo. Budo is a Way and therefore a discipline, a science, a technique, the essential principles of which can be found throughout the other disciplines.

One skilled in judo or aiki-do today is apparently not concerned with the spirit which fired the samurai; times have changed but the basic principles, the profound science of movements, actions, breathing, energy and tactics are immutable. These principles (many of which are still secret) are the very roots of the tree which lead to the martial arts we know today. In actual fact, what we see nowadays is a combination of all these principles.

From the sword to wisdom

The Western mind has great difficulty in imagining how the idea of the sword, which represents purely a weapon of death, can be connected to a concept of wisdom and, to a greater extent, to the notion of Way. Yet, the Way of the sword surpasses traditional wisdom to which we are accustomed, it is greater than the idea of meditation, of deep personal reflection, of the renunciation of the world, of self-denial and greater than the ascetic image it assumes. In its true definition, it embodies all the most essential steps to wisdom and, in a way, takes their meaning to its ultimate conclusion.

Of course, we cannot recreate the necessary conditions, and even so it would be extremely difficult to imagine what the definition and application of the Way of the sword could have been like in Japan. However, from writings that have come down to us and the tradition which has survived to this day in certain *Ryu*, we at least gain an approximate idea, a semblance of the significance of this Way.

By way of definition, we should not forget that the true meaning of the Way lies in application combined with total self-commitment.

Maniwa-Nen school.
Sword kata on the river bank.

THE WAY OF NATURE AND ORIGINAL ENERGY

Ki

Body and mind are two apparently separate entities. Yet the mind controls the body (a rule of budo). Internal awareness, real efficiency, the accomplishment of every action, all require the union of body and mind. The energy which effects this union is called *ki*. It obeys the mind which can direct it, cause it to concentrate on one area and make it flow.

Ki is the secret of all budo. It is impossible to progress in any form of martial art without first mastering ki. In aiki-do, it has become a fundamental understanding. Ki is understood to be either like original vital energy, or like breath or spirit.

The meaning behind these words lies in a single fact, for ki, the fundamental energy of the universe (which connects and relates all things) is also the true body of things in the subtle sense. From there on, it can combine with breath and spirit and, in turn, be the very emanation of breath and spirit.

Ki is life itself. As long as ki exists, life continues. When the vital energy disappears, life ceases. The control of ki therefore represents control over life, health, harmony, and therefore energy.

We must not forget that ki is a unifying force. Death is the end of ki and therefore the irreparable separation of body and mind. Conversely, the longer ki is retained in the body, the longer one's life. The Taoists in China have founded a method of prolonging life on this belief, of becoming immortal or of crossing the threshold of death while still alive. (In fact, it involves a long, complex asceticism intended to refine the body until it becomes an emanation of this energy.)

If ki gives at least spiritual immortality, this is because ki is the energy or original force which has been present ever since the creation of the universe and because this force is independent of time and space.

This concept explains why, as man is the emanation of universal nature, all consciousness stems from and returns to nature which is a common book for all mankind.

Master Otake of the Katori Shinto Ryu in meditation.

The hara and the vital point

How can ki be determined? How can one learn to feel it, use it, project it?

Sumo, karate, aiki-do all have rules for the use and mastery of ki. However, the disciplines of budo all agree on one point: mastery of the energy passes through the hara.

Mastery of the hara is often wrongly interpreted as mastery of the stomach. The hara can be represented by a circle, this being the centre of diffused energy. It is obvious that the centre of gravity is always low down. If the body is relaxed, the force sinks naturally to the nether regions of the body. This spot is

The subtle body's centres.
Illustration of the canals and chakras
of the subtle body according
to yoga. The hara is centred below the navel.

the hara, situated just less than 1 inch (2cm) below the navel. However, if the hara represents a circle, the centre is called seika-no-itten, or Vital Point.

This point is the true centre of equilibrium of ki, in other words of all vital energy in the body. Unless this is understood, aiki-do and its stunning power remains an enigma. This point is geometrically, in the spiritual and psychical sense, the spot where the laws of mind and body converge. It alone can ensure mental and physical coordination, and without this coordination all power is illusive and short-lived.

Concentration of the hara prior to kyudo practice. It is
the point of concentration which releases the arrow.

The laws of nature

There is no teaching worthy of its name which can ignore the laws of nature. The relationship between man and nature is complex. Broadmindedness and intuitive understanding are more instructive than words.

It is remarkable to see in China and Japan how the understanding of nature, or better still the natural laws, have throughout the ages been condensed into a single theme where life, religion, philosophy, exercise, martial arts, medicine, painting, architecture are all closely interwoven to the point where they are all complementary. In Japan, Shinto is no more than the expression of profound familiarity with nature and consequently an initiation into the relationship of cosmic laws. In China, Tao expresses a similar theme. Every race has interpreted the development of this fundamental awareness in its own way.

This understanding of nature does not distinguish between body and mind, present and future. The essence of everything is ONE. The universe is ONE. All philosophical distinctions, either moral or religious, which give a fragmented and analytical view of things, are vain and harmful within this concept.

The essence of things is not necessarily spiritual, nor is it material. The immanence of all things real – the famous 'here and now' – is in harmony with a deep respect and veneration of universal laws. When the holy feeling is born, it is not a rare and mystical outburst but a daily fact of life, an attitude which always embodies the individual in the Whole. Such a sentiment stems from the person's total participation in this universal reality with which he feels a profound harmony. This harmony is none other than life itself.

Life is in harmony with progress which expresses the law of alternation and also the vibration of the continuous and discontinuous. The dialectic, the mechanical, the quantitative, all that modern Western culture emanates, interrupt the natural progress of things and break the spontaneous order. Instead, abstract and conceptual systems are substituted. The rule of conduct and the implicit discipline of life no longer have a place; the natural hierarchy is missing, and this fact leads to a counter-nature, the result of which is conflict.

It is significant to see to what extent the idea of a discipline, or learning things for their own sake, exists in budo. The custom, practised by all the great masters from Musashi to Ueshiba, of going from one ryu to another challenging competitors in order to measure their own skills, has its limitation.

What happens when the master finds out that he really is the best? He gives up the struggle and the competition and tries to gain more knowledge. Often, for several years, asceticism and meditation take the place of combat, and sometimes illumination occurs – that is to say, at the peak of voluntary effort, an awareness of an involuntary force which is even greater and better and which, this time, has no desire to conquer the enemy, for there are no longer any opponents. The other man has become himself. Reality is no longer anything other than a play of mirrors reflecting exactly what it sees.

The illumination of the masters is this time the expression of a vision of the Whole, a fundamental experience eliminating all opposition. The interpenetration of all things, the indescribable movement of progression, the perception of a gap in time, the inexpressible waves of energy which are light, vibration and sound all at once, together demonstrate a force of life so powerful and so sudden that only the word love in its most absolute sense can describe it.

Such was the experience of Master Ueshiba. The orientals, reluctant to speak even of simple things, keep such experiences a guarded secret. But, in Japan, there is a whole area of secrecy concerning budo and a number of masters who carry on their solitary asceticism in their mountain refuge.

The five elements

Water, fire, wood, metal, earth all constitute another key to understanding. Everything we know stems from the alliance, opposition and transformation of these elements. They represent both force and substance. They are connected by bonds linking microcosm and macrocosm. They represent the beginning and end of all energy known to us. Budo is concerned with the rhythmic aspects of the elements which set up relationships between them. These rhythms are the deep-rooted principles of all

Master Nakano
shooting in his garden
in ceremonial dress.

things. That is why many of the masters learn all the arts of combat and familiarize themselves with all the different weapons, not because of an eclectic concern but driven on by the search for the principle which governs each discipline. To understand this principle is to have mastered the art.

All movement begins at a point and continues to infinity. In aiki-do, *happo undo* means exercise of the eight directions. One learns to extend the mind in the same direction as the body. One action depicts a circle – this circle is the universe. Ki starts from a vital point and increases as its force tends to augment its power, to infinity. Similarly, in kyudo, there is a saying: 'One shot, one life.' Master Awa said: 'The bowman pierces the sky with the end of his bow; at the other end is the earth, attached to a silk thread.' It all expresses profound universal harmony, fragile yet indestructible, which must also be the bowman's harmony.

The Way is there. It can be synonymous with breath, harmony and love. Desire, tension, anguish, wilfulness, fear, passion, etc., all come before the Way is reached; in other words, all that is human, too human, and all that is the ultimate in perception of the forms and realities of life. In this case, man is his own obstacle, the arrow cannot be fired. It stops at the target; man cannot be altered; the Way of budo, whose sole purpose in life is to achieve internal transformation, cannot be attained.

Demonstration of sword kata and kiai by
Master Takizo Higuchi, great master of the Maniwa Nen ryu.

THE WAY OF TACTICS

How can one bring oneself to shoot, to release the arrow, to allow movement to flow freely and spontaneously?

Internal transparence in the Way of budo means instantaneous equation between attack and defense. But how can such equality be achieved?

The weapon (sword, bokken, jo, bo, shinai, etc.) or the skill itself (aiki-do, karate, judo, etc.) form the basis of the tactics. From there, the rule is to perfect one's handling of the weapon, including thrusts and hits. The exercise becomes natural when practised over and over again. Movements and actions, which at first seemed difficult, flow freely and apparently without effort.

Rhythm

It is then that rhythm comes in. Every movement is a rhythm, just as in painting, music or poetry. If one is aware of the rhythm, it is possible to sense what is in rhythm and what is not. This new sense would be like a spontaneous master if only one were to heed it. A correct rhythm expresses proportion, balance, universal order. Rhythms reveal whether they are in conjunction or in opposition to each other. Work on rhythms is already a rule of life and in itself an understanding of harmony and discord, which explains exactly why the martial arts are constantly evolving and why the basic principles, revived and studied, have developed into new concepts from which new schools and teachings emerge.

When rhythm is achieved, the length of time a contest lasts is neither long nor short. The rhythm is timeless. It can appear to be slow or fleetingly quick. But neither its slowness nor fastness is expressed. A sword which cuts swiftly – explains Musashi – cuts nothing.

Sai against sword, fight by Master Shiokawa.

Seeing without looking = perceiving

'Seeing', said Musashi, 'is more important than looking.' There lies another rule of budo, which constantly advises one never to concentrate on the point of the sword (or shinai), the wrist, the action, the opponent's eyes or the target.

The rule is to see without seeing, to perceive without concentrating, to sense and not to parry or return an attack. The eyes which see are within one.

Perceiving the opponent

Every art consists of practising to the point at which the opponent becomes predictable, in other words when his intention to attack is perceived before the attack itself. In practice, one can guess the intended path of the weapon or opposing move.

This ability to perceive an attack is the essence of the development of a sixth sense. Its object is also to find out the opponent's rhythm and so to overcome him by imposing a different unfamiliar rhythm.

One shot, one hit

Another rule of budo expressed in the idea 'one shot, one life' is to make the first hit the decisive hit. This is also expressed by the term 'one rhythm'. One hit engages the whole being. That means that one must visualize the hit and the movement. The thrust has already taken place before one. The hit has already occurred. That is why it is said that victory precedes the winner.

In kendo, the kiai, the power given to the leap forward, the striking power of the shinai, are all coordinated into an intense and powerful rhythm in order that the first hit should be totally effective. It was once a rule of sword fighting too. (Here, we are far removed from the techniques of parade and defense practised by the glamorous sword virtuosos so dear to the West.)

Fighting several opponents at once

Master Ueshiba made this rule into an essential principle in aiki-do. Fighting several opponents is the same as fighting one. The tactics are either totally effective or not at all. If a great master of the sword was virtually insuperable whether confronted with 10 or 20 contestants at once, it was proof that he was using no special technique. On several occasions, Musashi put to flight or cut to pieces groups of samurai armed with swords, long spears and bows. He acted in such a way that he came out of the battle unscathed, without even a scratch. The rule says that opponents must not be permitted to lay a finger on the challenger.

This rule which is also of a tactical nature can be summed up: always dominate the opponent physically and psychologically, in space and time. Therefore, ascertain the best position afforded by the grounds, the position of the sun (or lights). It is said that victory comes to him who knows how to take the initiative of attack and knows, as it were, how to manipulate his opponent as he thinks fit. Attack the instant he attacks and prevent him from carrying out another attack or from considering a new tactic.

Removing the spirit

The way of tactics is very complex. In do, the object is not the destruction of the opponent, although we must not forget that every martial art can become a method of fighting, should the need arise, and be taken to extreme conclusions.

In do, the opponent becomes the partner, whilst in bugei, at one time, the aim more often than not was to destroy the opponent by all permissible methods or tactics. It was recommended that one should not only destroy the opponent but obliterate his 'spirit', to the extent, that is, of him losing any wish to fight again. This is why many beaten warriors, whose life had been spared, became Zen monks.

Master Takano, the great master of kendo, said one should see the opponent as one sees a mountain in the distance. This demonstration took place in the Hachiman Shinto sanctuary in Kamakura.

Victory by any means

This rule does not mean that all methods of gaining victory are permissible but that it is not sufficient to study just a few techniques in depth. The result of practice and an effective voluntary training is nothing compared to global vision and true internal mastery. A master can win with any weapon, even with no weapon at all. That is why it is advisable to beware of ryu and techniques which are too precise and which by their fragmented abstract training give the pupil a false idea as to his true potential.

The opposition of ryu, superiority of one weapon over another, is from this point of view merely theoretical. As the saying goes, truth mocks truth.

The start is like the finish: the Way without a way

When tactics are surpassed, in other words perfectly assimilated, the man resembles the novice he was when he knew nothing. He regains the same state of innocence. Now, like before, he is unaware of the rules. He has reached the 'Way without a way': the ultimate reality or, as expressed by Lao Tseu and many Zen masters since: 'The way which is the Way is not the way, the name which is the name is not the name.'

The void

Musashi says: 'Consider the Way as a void. In this void there is good and no evil. Intelligence is ''being''; principles are ''being''; the Ways are ''being''. But the mind is a void.'

79

Sword training beside a river. The kiai is about to be released. (Maniwa Nen ryu).

CONSCIOUS ENERGY AND THE DEVELOPMENT OF THE POWERS

Vital energy is one. It is the mother of the universe, permeating all things. This vital energy is the true goodness given to us at birth. Yet a lifetime can go by without this energy ever demonstrating exceptional powers. On the contrary, knowing how to direct it and put it to good use means achieving results which can seem miraculous.

In itself, energy is neither good nor bad. It is above all what the mind and the conscience make of it. If the mind is positive, the energy will itself become positive and creative – a bad negative mind will similarly develop a negative energy.

In budo, many forms of art or exercise exist, the aim of which is to direct and use this energy. Here are a few examples.

Kokyu or the power to direct vital energy

Masters of aiki-do or judo usually say that they can tell whether or not a pupil has kokyu as soon as he walks on to the tatame. Word for word, kokyu means the use of ki (vital energy) or use of the body according to ki. In other words, when someone is gifted with a strong positive energy, his kokyu, or use of this vital power, is expressed through him. Mastery of his actions in thrusts shows a strong kokyu (when others are guided by one's own kokyu, the expression used is kokyu-nage or kokyu ho).

The kiai

All the martial arts have their own cry or 'kiai', often quite terrifying, which is apparently the expression of the sudden release of energy. A romantic interpretation of the kiai has made it famous in the West under the name of 'cry that kills'. In actual fact, the kiai is a 'setting up of wave lengths' between two contestants. He who has the greatest amount of subtle energy (ki) makes it known by the kiai. It is undeniable that, just for a fraction of a second, a sort of inhibition occurs, just long enough to strike the opponent. It is also said that by the kiai some masters are able to paralyse a bird on a branch, to make it fall at their feet even. In this case, the technique used is to make the kiai the vehicle for a sort of hypnotic energy, just sufficient to immobilize the bird for a brief moment.

So, the kiai must come from the stomach, that is from the centre of true energy; if it comes only from the throat, it is ineffective: in this case, nothing more than a guttural sound is emitted. In fact, the kiai is the art or science of using ki or energy.

The expression 'vital energy force', or subtle power within things, comes up constantly throughout this book and means that all forms of life, especially budo, are an application of this energy.

'Vibration existed both at the beginning and the end; between the two, the earth and the universe have lived.' On this ancient Shinto thought rests a profound esoteric understanding. The vibration (impersonal state of energy) is seen as a sound in the mind (specific state of energy). To know the power of sound is to make energy vibrate, in other words to make life itself vibrate.

All things can be explained by sound or rather by the vibration modes of sound. This ancient knowledge, fully confirmed since by numerous scientific applications (power of sound over plants and animals in particular) enables one to understand how the kiai can be so much more than a blood-thirsty cry and can express its energy in all areas of existence. In this case, the kiai can also be silent; above all it implies an active decision from the mind, such that the strongest uses his influence over the weakest.

The kiai is controlled by the hara, or what the Japanese call *fukushiki kokyu*, in other words deep breathing from the stomach. Breathing exercises train one to do this.

The kiai is definitely the result of a science which embodies a command of breathing, as well as of the mind. The spirit controls ki which makes the hara vibrate. The kiai in a way projects mental, physical and psychical energy. That is why the word KIAI is the opposite of AIKI.

Master Higuchi uttering the kiai.

Iai beside the sea between the very great master (of iai), Tomihara, and Master Shiokawa, not far from Shimonoseki (Kyushu).

Kime

Kime is the gathering of all the body's physical and psychical forces in one spot. Kime can be compared to a laser beam which pierces and travels through any object the moment it comes to it. It is said that a master from Kagoshima who one day wanted to show the effectiveness of kime, gave the following demonstration: he suspended a bamboo stick on two paper discs held up by two razor blades. One scarcely had to touch this fragile construction to make it collapse. The master took a wooden sword or bokken and, after concentrating, he struck a sharp blow in the direction of the bamboo but stopped within a hair's breadth of it. The bamboo split.

Kime, in fact, has a power of penetration. Although the blow stops short, the kime continues. In this way, some ryu teach people to break pieces of wood with the bokken. The wood must break without having been touched.

Similarly, Aoki, the master of karate, from the Shotokai school, carries out the following experiment with his pupils: he places five cushions on the stomach of one of the pupils and strikes a blow without using his concentration or physical strength. The pupil feels nothing. The second time, the master concentrates and the pupil feels the force go through his stomach in spite of the five cushions. In another experiment, the pupil can also feel the effect of kime from behind a door.

Development of a sixth sense and the power to anticipate an attack

The power to anticipate an attack was once the key to knowing whether one had the

makings of a true samurai. This explains the scene in the film 'The Seven Samurai' in which warriors are defending the village. The samurai who receives them in the centre of a room has taken the precaution of concealing a man who surprises each warrior as he enters with a harsh blow from a stick. Only the true samurai anticipate the attack and are prepared for it. The others go off with no further explanation.

The power to anticipate an attack comes from the development of a sixth sense. The sixth sense, sometimes wrongly confused with the third eye, enables one to grasp the assailant's intentions, and so to forestall or guide his movements. Such a faculty can be likened to the power of a man with two good eyes compared to that of a blind man.

The human race has undoubtedly lost the use of this sixth sense which the majority of animals have kept. It was the awakening, the gift of feeling the subtle relationship which exists between the animal, vegetable and human kingdoms. It is probable that the pineal gland, situated in the brain at the base of the diencephalon, played a decisive role in the unification of the faculties of the mind and the use of the sixth sense.

Master Ueshiba Morihei suffered surprise attacks many times, either from behind if he was seated, or whilst he was asleep or walking along. One day, several thugs attacked him and were all repulsed. 'Before someone attacks me', said the master, 'his ki comes towards me. If I dodge it and his body follows the ki, I only have to touch him lightly to make him fall to the ground.'

Men of the mountain and the search for the powers

We have seen the importance and the sacred role of the mountain in Shinto, which explains why numerous masters, in the

83

course of their life, retreat into the mountains for several years to meditate and undergo a physical and spiritual asceticism.

It happens that the man of the mountain (Yama-Otoke) is also a sennin or sort of yogi or hidden ascete living alone, eating herbs, sweet chestnuts and wild fruit. Such men, lightly clad, even in freezing cold winters, develop apart from their ability to resist cold all sorts of natural or parapsychical powers. Many legends exist on the subject of their powers, some quite extraordinary (such as the power of levitation and of moving in space, the power of foresight, etc.). It can happen that masters in martial arts meet these ascetes and themselves acquire certain cognition, or that the ascetes can practise one of the budo disciplines in surprising and unexpected ways. As it is extremely difficult to meet such men, we must be content to echo a very ancient tradition which, in view of the number and the quality of the witnesses, would seem to be worth believing.

Many things seem to us extraordinary or inexplicable. Without going into the kind of Japanese or Hindu romanticism which was prevalent in the West during the thirties and which seems to be returning, let us say that traditional Japan, like ancient China, today expresses a rare science: that of man and his fundamental nature, that of the universe and its cosmic powers. From Shinto to Zen, from budo to the ascetes, there are buddhist sects with popular traditions, a thousand spiritual manners or occult ways of interpreting this relationship. Suffice to say that there is a lot to learn for him who cares to search. Even today, Japan is above all the country of the invisible. That which is visible is only there to conceal its true identity more effectively. Experienced in this double act and, subconsciously or not, preferring it, the Japanese have more than anyone mastered the art of making one wait, of detracting one from the goal, or of showing the complete opposite of what one came to find.

The present generation of Japanese, joined to its distant past by many subconscious bonds and raised within constricting social structures from which it often tries to escape, has made tradition a taboo subject. Why speak of what is inexplicable? And what is inexplicable?

Maybe it is the sentiment interpreted by a Zen master 500 years ago:
It is proclaimed that the only Thought
was, is and will be.

A lake on Hokkaido.

Like a cloud veils the moon,
so matter veils
the face of Thought.

Meditation and purification

It is common to see Japanese masters undergo a long solitary retreat into the mountains to meditate. To go up a mountain which is sacred in the Shinto concept is to renew the most important elements with the forces of nature, in a way to enter into a contract with the divine.

The mountain demands deprivation and self-sacrifice. The powerful energies which

man finds there regenerate the being, making him positive (yang). The more the body frees itself, the more it receives the vibration of celestial energies.

In other words, faithful to tradition and ancient knowledge, a master of budo by necessity feels the need to recharge his energy and this involves solitary meditation, the cold, icy baths, meditation beneath a waterfall, fasting, etc., all of which facilitate the acquisition of fresh energies and often stimulate a profound internal illumination and transformation.

The start of the new year is the time when many Japanese undertake *Misogi harai* – a collection of purification processes in the physical, moral and spiritual sense. The main object is the same as before: the toxins which pollute the body, the spirit and the soul must be expelled whatever their nature, otherwise the being becomes opaque; the fundamental vibration of the universe can no longer get through to him. Shinto tradition celebrates renewal rites each year at the beginning of January.

Man-grass-vegetation and *man-developing-to infinity,* as Shinto points out, are two ways of defining the relationship which is both antagonistic and complementary between mind and body. A collection of practices called gyo rests on this concept, whereby man, recognizing the unity of body and mind in himself, becomes at the same time at one with cosmic and universal nature.

Tsuba

Handguards or tsuba have been the object of remarkable craftsmanship in Japan, making them into works of art sought after by a great number of collectors. (The slots on either side were for inserting smaller swords: kozuka or wakizashi.) (Double page overleaf)

85

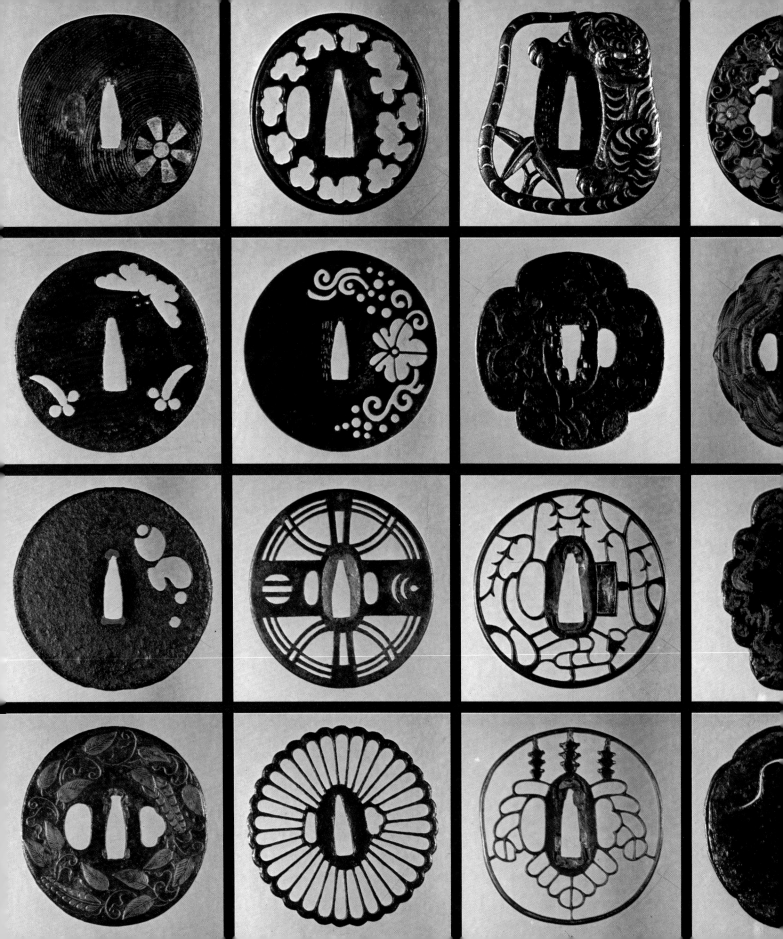

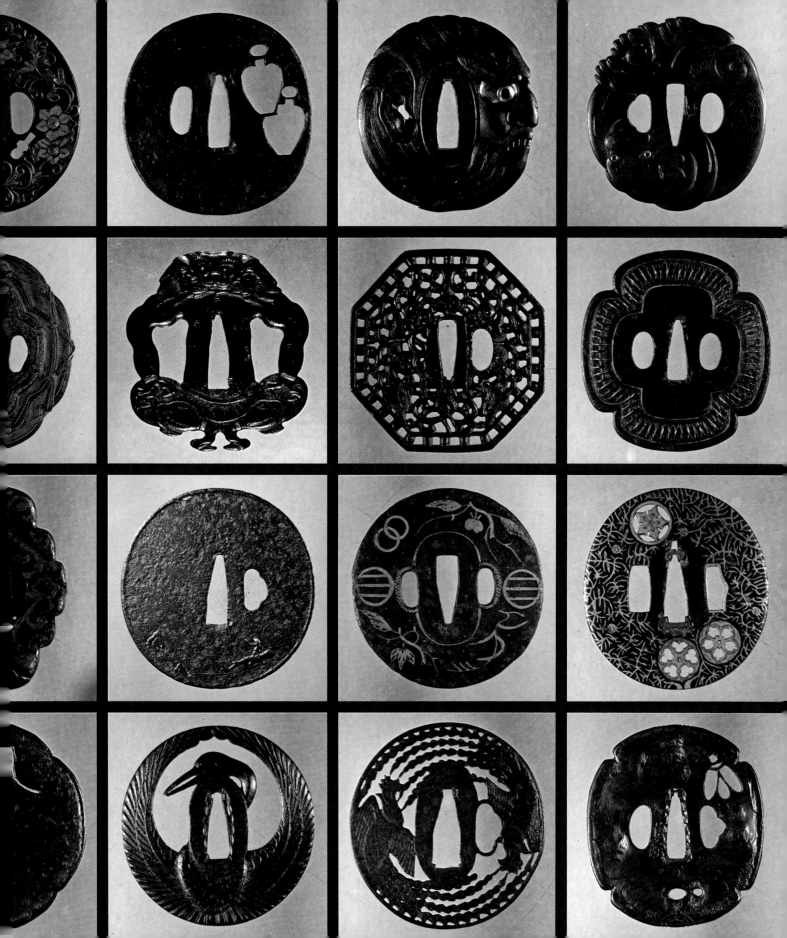

Three great masters demonstrate iai, or the art of drawing a sword.

The idea is that in such a communion there exists an extraordinary vital and subtle force. Our access to it is prevented by the physical, mental or moral impurities which cloud our body and put up a sort of veil between us and this vital energy. Hence the need to purify body and soul.

There are numerous methods of misogi, for individuals or groups. The group method is often preferred because it emanates a collective force which permits one to accomplish one's own misogi more effectively.

Understanding and the Way of chivalry

There is no difference between understanding and the Way of chivalry. They are interwoven and interdependent, like the bow and arrow, the target being internal progress.

The following verses by a Japanese master summarize and clarify all that has been said so far:

I have no parents;
I make the earth and sky my parents.
I have no home;
In the depths of my soul (saika tanden) [1] I make my home.

I have no divine power;
I make integrity my power.
I have no means;
Humility is my means.
I have no magic power;
Internal force is my magic.
I have neither life, nor death;
I make the Eternal my life and my death.
I have no body;
I make courage my body.
I have no eyes;
The flash of light and there are my eyes.
I have no ears;
Sensitivity serves as my ears.
I have no limbs;
Instantaneous movement, there are my limbs.
I have no law;
I make my own protection my law.
I have no strategy;
Freedom to kill and freedom to give back life (sakkatsu jizai), there is my strategy.
I have no purpose;
Opportunity is my purpose (kisan= I seize the opportunity).
I have no miracle;
Just law is my miracle.

[1] Saika tanden, or the hara, cannot be translated. It expresses the centre of energy, the stomach, the Vital Point, all in one.

I have no principle;
Adaptability to all circumstances (rinkioken),
there is my principle.
I have no tactics;
I make existence and the void (kyojitsu) my
tactics.
I have no talent;
I make a quick mind (toi sokumyo) my talent.
I have no enemy;
I make irresponsibility my enemy.
I have no armour;
I make benevolence and uprightness my armour.
I have no castle;
The immutable spirit (fudoshin) is my castle.
I have no sword;
From the state which is above and beyond,
from thought (mushin) I make my sword.

In this way, moral strength and rectitude are the expression of wisdom. The force of desire is the only obstacle to the accomplishment of desire. In fact, it is the alliance of the voluntary and the involuntary (the hard way and the natural way), which stimulates both life (or death) and the double victory: over oneself and over others.

The masters, the secret and the refusal of education

It is clear that the old traditions or ryu strove to keep their knowledge a closely guarded secret. The tactics and secrets particular to each teaching, and the rivalry between the ryu and the clans justified such secrecy.

Until very recently, not only was it prohibited to film or photograph these ryu but even to watch the training of their pupils. Formerly, when a master wanted to test the superiority of another ryu, he had to send a challenge to its master. Then a sword fight could take place. If it so happened that the loser was spared by his opponent and that he was the one who had issued the challenge, the disgrace he suffered was so great that he often committed hara-kiri. This shows the importance of the secret techniques of these ryu which frequently closed down when the last master died. As for spiritual education, nowadays it is only given to the initiated in exceptional cases.

Before every contest or training session, Master Takizo Higuchi, together with the members of his school, pays hommage to the kami at a small Shinto altar.

Old master from the Maniwa-Nen ryu.

There is a considerable difference between the modern dojo and the old traditions, which is scarcely noticeable to us because we only see the martial arts of Japan through what we have learnt from the familiar aspects of judo, karate or aiki-do. Nowadays, what used to make the old bugei (martial arts) seem strange to us has been polished and made to conform to what we ideally expect of these disciplines. An abundance of literature exists, though, which builds up, with the help of thousands of different accounts and anecdotes, a sort of imagery, often quite ingenious, illustrating the exploits of yesterday and today, from the ancient samurai to the masters of the modern dojo.

The Japanese are careful not to contradict or to intervene in order to counteract this sort of new romanticism surrounding competition and efficacy. What they would have to say is so far removed from what we are capable of understanding, that they use the opposite of this imagery to protect their secret training, if this is still possible. So it is in Japan, not only with what concerns the martial arts but with all the traditional Ways: the art of the potter, No or kabuki actors, ancient musicians and all the traditional skills in general. Behind its ultra-modern exterior, ancient Japan is silent, and instruction in the true teachings is only ever given to very small groups of people.

It is therefore very difficult for Westerners, and even for the Japanese themselves, to gain access to the true traditional sources in Japan. Moreover, the traditional Japanese spirit does not prove the need to teach or explain things the way we do, by using a language of concepts and analysis. The teaching flows from practice or impregnation. Oral explanations are only given to back up this teaching, and even so are used very sparingly.

That explains why there are no fundamental Japanese books on the martial arts and the teachings of the old schools; documents, films or even photographs are just as rare or non-existant. If we were not at a time when certain doors are visibly opening, it is probable that, for generations to come, the essential elements of these teachings would remain hidden, even in their most simple forms.

In fact, the secret itself is less important than the accurate passing on of information. It is the custom that all traditional Japanese ryu, whatever their field – theatre, music, pottery, crafts or martial arts – pass on the essential elements of their theories through the centuries by way of one person. This person was usually the son of the master, or the best pupil, who thus became his adopted son and was entitled to the same respect.

The secret of the teaching also clung to the fact that popularization of the knowledge is absolutely contrary to all traditional concepts. He who wished to be taught, first had to prove what this teaching signified for him and the price he was able to pay for it in spiritual and human terms.

'Your Western mind', a great master of kendo, Kosei Takano, told me, 'is eager to understand and explain everything. In fact, when a man tries to express what he thinks he has understood, he is like an invalid. Words are his prison.'

The great masters never explain what they know. A pupil must be elevated to the peak of his potential by his inward intuition alone. He must act with his mind much more than with his hands. He anticipates what conforms to the universal harmony of things. He who becomes a master captures this harmony like a sort of music inherent in his being; his presence of mind and balance are such that he can detect instantly anything which does not conform to the harmony. Furthermore, he must rise above the desire to win and the fear of death. Whatever happens, his inner state must be like a calm sea. The sword which cuts, breaks the disharmony which is before him.

All the martial arts are based on this spirit of nonteaching, or the refusal to apply methods of analysis or instruction which are insufficient and elementary in relation to what has to be understood. Nonteaching is therefore the only teaching which allows the inner comprehension to be free without having to face subjective and unsatisfactory definitions of words.

BUGEI AND BUDO

At the time of the samurai, bugei meant 'art of war' and the fighting skills intended, above all, for use and efficiency in battle. Bushido law, covering in depth the techniques of a spiritual understanding and code of conduct, completed the meaning of bugei.

The term *jutsu* (synonymous with skill) is added to bugei. There are about 23 bugei (including kyujutsu: the art of bow and arrows, kenjutsu: the art of sword fighting, iaijutsu: the art of drawing the sword from the scabbard, etc.) In the Meiji era (1868-1912), all forms of martial arts, begining to lose their offensive character, took the name budo – thus relating them to the traditional teaching of Japanese arts associated with peace and serenity. So, we get sado (or chado): the art of tea, kwado (or kado): the art of flowers, ido: the art of natural medicine; here *do* means the Way of harmony. Bowmanship expresses this idea of peace and thus became kyudo, the art of sword handling kendo and similarly all the *do* words already known to us: aiki-do, judo, karate-do, etc.

Budo means the martial arts (from bu meaning war and do, Way), or better still the 'Way of the warrior', in the chivalrous sense. In other words, budo gives a humanist significance to the martial arts. The spiritual use made of weapons is more important than the weapon itself. (So, in karate, it is appropriate to specify which type is practised, for example karate-do or karate-jutsu.)

Sword training (Maniwa-Nen ryu).

However, if there is a fundamental distinction between jutsu and do, one can see that originally the fighting technique always involved a situation in which the man was having to defend his life, and therefore being or trying to be the strongest when confronted by the enemy. The need for skill and the training of the inner man went together. To be freed from the fear of death, to preserve one's serenity and mastery (zanshin) at all costs were certainly not qualities which could easily be acquired without a lifetime's commitment. Therefore, there is a whole range of meanings which are too often simplified due to superficial literary knowledge, by making the way of do far too spiritual and by rejecting bugei-jutsu as if it were an illness from which one has mercifully recovered.

If there is a difference, it relates most of all to the rather vehement application of the traditional ways to sport and competition. There again, the thought needs explaining, for whenever an art is applied to a set of rules, distortions occur. However, between a rigid approach and realism, which takes into account the all round enrichment to be gained from aiki-do, judo, karate, kendo, etc., there is still room for the law of natural selection which comes between quantity and quality.

Shinto and Zen

It is customary to think that the Japanese masters are all inspired by the philosophy of Zen Buddhism. Far from it, all the dojo and all

make a very honest living. The masters of the old ryu, true to the spirit of the samurai who refused to handle or to have anything whatsoever to do with money, all have a second trade which permits them to earn their living. The teaching they give is of course a personal undertaking and their dedication to the tradition which they continue to hand down is entirely free of charge.

anese ryu are inspired by
pirit. A small Shinto shrine
er every dojo. When Zen
de its presence felt, it super-
practice which is original and

mains unclean

e old masters actually have a
and live deep in the coun-
fact that they are scattered
apan and far from the large
r greatest protection. On the
1 Tokyo, most of the masters of
s have enough pupils, who are
tend to their master's needs, to

THE SPIRIT OF ZEN

The word Zen is a derivative of the sanskrit 'Dhyana' and comes from the Chinese 'chan-na' meaning meditation. A legend says that Buddha passed the rules down to Kasyapa, his favourite pupil. After that, 27 patriarchs continued the teaching until the time of Bodhidharma who came to China from India around the year 600 and became the first Chinese Chan patriarch (Chinese Zen was called Chan).

Historically, Zen was introduced to Japan around the 13th century, as a reaction against different forms of Buddhism which had been taught in Japan since the 6th century and which had become progressively weak. That is why Mr Bernard Franck has no hesitation in saying that Zen is a sort of integrationist reaction against the temptations of ease which could be found in the amidist doctrine.[1] In practice, the effects of the Zen doctrine had considerable influence on Japan. Its arrival coincided with the founding of Japanese feudalism which dates from the end of the 12th century (it was then that the warrior class, by profession, rose to the top).

What is Zen?

It is possible to describe all that Zen is not: it is neither a system of ideas, nor metaphysics, nor religion. It is not encumbered with dogmas, nor with beliefs, symbols, temples or monastic vows. In Zen, there is nothing to

[1] Buddhism lacked an element of warmth and comfort, offering hope of a happy beyond, so Amidism was born and the worship of the Buddha Amida.

seek, nor any merit to be gained. There is no way, no faith is required, no saviour is awaited, no paradise is promised; no choice is offered, nor any attainment.

A monk, Superior of a Zen monastery, wanted to appoint his successor. He placed a pitcher in front of him and invited each of the other monks to say a few words about the pitcher. They all stretched their wits to describe the pitcher but the master did not seem to be in the least bit satisfied. Last of all came the cook. He hardly deigned to set eyes on the pitcher, but kicked it violently, causing it to shatter, then turned his back and went out. At last, the master's face lit up: the cook was the one who was chosen.

This story (koan) signifies that in Zen nothing exists. There is no question of describing the pitcher because neither pitcher, nor spirit, nor Buddha, nor any being, nor any thing has fundamental reality. That is why 'Kill the Buddha' is a well-known precept in Zen.

So, Zen is a stone thrown into the lake of appearances in order to disturb the Void of all things. Although the essence of reality is the ultimate goal sought by Zen, as this reality is nameless (that is of the same essence as the Absolute which is both indescribable and incommunicable), it is this Reality which Zen purports to understand, above any other method involving analytical reason.

That is why Zen explains nothing. To define a doctrine would make one a prisoner of that doctrine, whilst that which exists appears like a flash and disappears just as fast. At the same time, an observant person is conscious of a comprehension or momentary enlightenment which is known as 'satori'.

The idea of the Void can be described thus: if one imagines that man's life is like a knotted rope, Zen suggests that man should not add to the number of knots, nor increase his knowledge or various powers, but on the contrary unravel all the knots in the rope, to

No theatre

The great tradition of the No theatre is also a secret tradition passed down to us from the 15th century by Zeami.

Alone on the stage, the *shite* 'the one who acts' plays the leading role.

The tea ceremony (or chanoyu) is equal to Zen meditation, carried out with the aim of achieving spiritual calm and serenity.

make it straight and smooth, just as it was originally. That is why in Zen the Void is the opposite of nothingness. The sense of deity which Zen confers on man means that everything already exists within us and that it is sufficient to eliminate all the things which obscure true understanding in order to reestablish contact with this understanding.

It is appropriate to note that a modern physicist is more capable than anyone of understanding this reasoning. In the final analysis, he now knows that no man can ever renew the order of the creation from a single molecule. On the contrary, the more the infinitesimal is explored, the greater the number of different fields of energy which open up before one. So much so that the universe, in the image of the electron of which it is composed, is nothing more than a field of probabilities, according to Louis de Broglie's definition.

In the current order of life, the difficulty lies in learning not to put up a screen in front of what exists: in permitting movement to flow, words to be uttered, the true substance of life to emerge. In real life, the followers of Zen put forward a method of meditation, apparently absurd, which they call the 'koan'. This is a formula which goes against all conventions and all our deep-rooted culture, precisely because it tends to reject all intellectual and rational judgement. For instance, a monk when asked, 'How can my hand be the hand of the Buddha?' replies, 'By playing the lute by moonlight.' Or 'How can I get away from the spoken word and the silence since they both belong to the world of the relative and the absolute?' Reply: 'I think of the partridges chattering amongst the fragrant flowers.' In fact, famous monks have built up a whole set of 'koan' literature based on these preposterous answers, on which monks are still expected to meditate.

The oldest Zen poem begins thus:

The perfect way (Tao) is not a hard one, except that it avoids choice.
It is only when you stop loving and start hating that all can be clearly understood.
A minute difference is enough to divide heaven and earth.
If you wish to find the unclouded truth, do not concern yourself with right and wrong.
Conflicts with right and wrong are a sickness of the mind.

Zen monks in meditation.

Zen stories

Hakuin (1685-1768) was one of the greatest Zen masters. One day, an important lord came to ask him: 'What is hell and what is paradise?' Instead of answering, Hakuin insulted him: 'What a stupid lord you are! Narrow-minded too! You do not even know the doctrine of Buddhism. How can the vassals be expected to obey such an ass? Scatterbrain!' The lord contained himself at first but when he could not take any more, he drew his sword. Hakuin stepped back and then ran in all directions while continuing to insult the lord who pursued him. In the end Hakuin was cornered, with the lord's sword raised above his head. Preparing to strike him down, the lord said: 'There you are, Hakuin!' At that moment Hakuin cried out: 'That is hell!' The lord hesitated a moment. Immediately, Hakuin cried out: 'That is paradise!'[1]

[1] Masumi Shibata, *Zen Masters of Japan,* published (in French) by Maisonneuve and Larose.

Yi Sencan: Xinxin Ming

An extremely wise person once met a Zen master. Immediately, he prepared to ask him all sorts of questions. The Zen master poured him some tea and continued pouring until the cup was full, then went on pouring so that the cup overflowed. Surprised, the wise man observed: 'Master, can you not see that the cup is overflowing?' 'Well', said the master, 'how do you expect me to teach you anything when your mind is like this cup? You came with your mind too full of things, not to learn but to criticize and argue. So I have nothing to say to you, I can teach you nothing.'

One day, a Zen monk, Tong Yin-Fong, was pushing a cart. He stopped before his master who was resting in the middle of the path with his legs outstretched.

'Master, kindly move your legs out of the way', said Tong.

'I never move my legs when they are stretched out', said the master.

'And I never go backwards when I am pushing my cart forwards', replied Tong. So saying, he pushed his cart over the master's legs, wounding him.

Later on, having gathered the monks together in the meditation room, the master advanced, brandishing an axe.

'Let the one who wounded my legs with his cart earlier on step forward', he said.

So Tong came forward, knelt before the master and stretched out his neck, whereupon the master laid down the axe.

A student who wished to learn about Zen had the following conversation with his master:

Student: 'Where do we come from and where do the 10,000 things and the 10,000 beings come from?'

Master: 'Everything comes from the Cosmic Mind. Everything is the Cosmic Mind.'

Student: 'Where are we going? Where are the 10,000 things and the 10,000 beings heading?'

Master: 'Everything goes back to the Cosmic Mind. Everything is the Cosmic Mind.'

Student: 'Where does the Cosmic Mind come from? Where is it going?'

The master took off his slipper and struck the student a heavy blow on the head.

CALLIGRAPHY OR THE SEVENTH MARTIAL ART

Most of the masters of the martial arts practise calligraphy which is in itself considered to be the seventh martial art. For is not the ability to make the stroke flow naturally, to let the brush move freely across a thin piece of paper, also a superior struggle of the most testing kind? The spontaneous stroke of the brush is reminiscent of the quick free thrust of the sword or the freedom of the arrow fired effortlessly. Wherever there is distress, worry or uneasiness, there can be no perfect freedom or swiftness of action.

Calligraphy which is the art of drawing characters with the tip of a brush dipped in ink, requires a profound serenity. Here again, harmony comes from control over breathing and movement. Introduced into Japan from China about 1300 years ago, calligraphy was then the art of transcribing Chinese ideographs (kanji in Japanese). Nowadays, both kanji and kana (Chinese ideographs transcribed phonetically) are used.

It is said that internal serenity drives the brush. The brush in effect interprets the deepest part of the subconscious. The 'wisdom of the eye' is what relates the characters to each other as though assembling the movable and the immutable, the ego to the 10,000 things in the universe, the present to the timeless.

Calligraphy and Zen painting (sumi-e = painting with ink)

The student who wishes to learn calligraphy begins by studying an ideograph. He draws it once, 50 times, 100 times, even 300 times. One works from top to bottom and from left to right, always in the same direction. The movement cannot be reversed. If one ideograph consists of six or seven strokes, each one requires a particular pressure. The sign is repeated until total spontaneity is achieved, completely free from thought . . . spontaneity and not automatism of movement which is contrary to the object of the exercise. In calligraphy (as in the martial arts), the space between the lines is what matters. It is this space which gives the signs their beauty. In Zen painting, we find this same need for pressure and spontaneity. Here, we see the result of the movement of the brush and the ink on the paper. The brush is dipped in *encre de chine*. The special quality paper is very fine and absorbant. The brush hardly needs to touch the paper to make a large blob. Therefore, the hand must skim or fly across the paper without stopping. Thought is free. It is the hand which thinks and acts.

There are traditional designs in sumi-e: bamboo canes, figures, houses, landscapes. It is fitting to avoid excesses, to strive for economy of strokes and resources, to create the greatest possible emotion with the maximum solemnity. An old master of sumi-e said that the day he managed to say everything with a dot, he would have earned his life, present and future. He called this dot 'the immovable vibrating point'.

In the universe, everything is movement and vibration. This universal vibration is identical to a point and this point contains all the energy of the universe: past, present and future.

Calligraphy expressing the idea of the Void, by the Zen master, Taisen Deshimaru.

The Way of the bow and

the horse

The subconscious action of Master Anzawa

Kneeling in the seiza position, Master Anzawa, the greatest master of bowmanship in Japan, collects his thoughts. The noise from the nearby town can be heard in the dojo at the bottom of his garden, but he hears nothing. He has created a silence within himself. With movements in which breathing and deliberation are in harmony, he kneels down with the bow on his left touching the ground. His feet in tightly fitting white stockings (tabi) slide softly on the shiny wooden floor of the dojo. It is like watching some sort of choreography display by the No theatre company, in which the slightest action seems to last an eternity; then he gets up, carries out various actions, slides forward, bares his left shoulder, kneels down and remains still. He then takes hold of his bow, positions the first white-fletched arrow, takes a second arrow which he will hold in his fingers whilst preparing to shoot the first. Slowly, the axis of the bow is raised to head level and turns to face the target. The unity of tension in the bow and inward concentration is complete at the moment of true accomplishment, the arrow is loosed, like a flower opening, accompanied by a short sharp cry – the kiai.

For a moment, the master's eye remains trained on the target, for the arrow continues spiritually; it is the symbol of energy itself; nothing can stand in its way. 'One arrow, one life', says Master Anzawa; he is 83. Then comes a gradual unwinding, the point of concentration which released the arrow is relaxed, the master is himself again. After shooting a second arrow, he will slide to the back of the dojo as before, place his bow before him, bow to it, almost touching the floor with his forehead. A perfect action will have taken place.

Between the moment he picked up his bow and when he shot his first arrow, a long time elapsed, during which the master eliminated from his mind all that was not connected with the thought of the action; inward concentration affected the alchemy of the unity: man, bow, arrow, target were as one. At the peak of concentration, the arrow flies spontaneously, like a child who inadvertently drops something in all innocence: it is the perfect involuntary action which accomplishes the loose; in addition, the goal is attained.

Master Anzawa

Master Anzawa, small in stature, seemed enormous when shooting. For him, kyudo was virtually a holy act.

The great master of kyudo: Anzawa.

Master Anzawa who died in February 1970 at the age of 83 was one of the last great masters of kyudo. To see him shoot was to understand visually what he said: 'One must always aim beyond the target. One must aim a long way: our whole life, our whole spirit travels with the arrow. And when the arrow has been fired, it is never the end.' Thus he explained the very essence of Zen Buddhism.

The bow carrier, during Master Nakano's ceremonial act. The Japanese bow varies in length according to its use: target practice, from varying distances, use in battle, or on ceremonial occasions. Learning archery first involves learning the actions and the positioning of the body. Only after a lengthy preparation is the pupil allowed to face the target. To aim at the target above all means achieving harmony in the shot, rather than accuracy, which is an additional feat.

THE WAY OF THE BOW AND THE HORSE

The Way of the bow and the horse did not originate in Japan. Chinese bowmen have taught it since the 11th century, using different bows for different occasions (fighting, hunting, shooting on foot, shooting from horseback, etc.)

But it was at the time of the Taira and Minamoto clans in the second half of the 12th century that the 'Way of the bow and the horse' took on its full meaning. The bow became the principal weapon, to the extent that a warrior was designated 'he who carries the bow and arrow'.

Origin of the Japanese bow

The oldest known evidence of bows goes back to drawings found on the walls of prehistoric caves or caverns.

The earliest asymmetrical bow found in Japan dates from the time of Kofun-bunka-jidai (3rd or 4th century AD). It was found near Lake Tokos, in the province of Nara, in the very heart of Yamato, the cradle of Japan. After examining it, the experts deduced that it was powerful, was strung in the opposite way to the resting position of the curve and, judging from a few traces of bands, must have been laminated. This discovery is important as it destroys the simplistic tendency to regard ancient bows as being of primitive conception, both in shape and substance.

Two main factors have affected the development of the Japanese bow: density of material – with the introduction of *take* (a type of very hard bamboo exclusive to Japan), and application.

Originally, the basic material used was a shrub which would explain the bow's asymmetry: the upper part of the shrub being weaker in effect that the very much stronger lower part. So, the Japanese would have decentered the grip in order to concentrate most of the power on the strongest part.

The length of the bow is determined by its use: target practice (from varying distances), hunting, use in battle or on ceremonial occasions. Later on, the combination of laminating materials and the choice of base material permitted variations in power. It is

Drawings after Hokusai depicting the legend of Tamemoto who, during the war between the Taira and the Minamoto sank a ship with a single arrow.

107

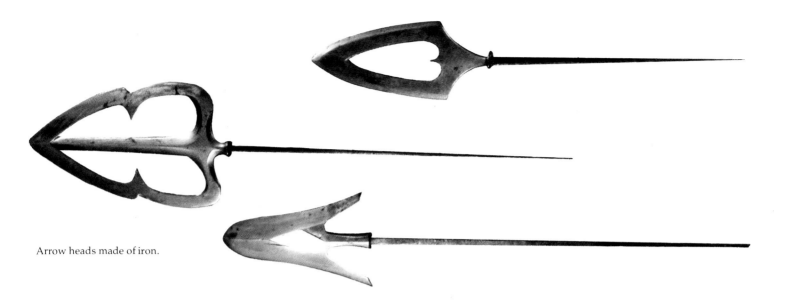

Arrow heads made of iron.

This statue is the guardian of a Shinto temple. These 'guardians' (always two) are armed with bows and arrows. If their statues have been animated, that is to say inhabited by the spirit of the kami, their alcoves become veritable shrines.

interesting to note that the *take* found in Kanto (Tokyo) and in Yamato (Kyoto-Nara) possess intrinsic qualities appropriate for ceremonial bows, whilst the *take* from Kagoshima (Kyushu) is particularly suited to fighting bows.

During the Mongol invasion in the 13th century, the Japanese discovered the Mongol bows, made of a fairly slender core of pliable wood, reinforced with horn plating on both the belly and the back. After that two or three layers of ox tendons were added and the whole thing glued and left in a mould so that the bow would take on its final shape. The Japanese exploited this method of manufacture by reinforcing the *take* with different types of wood: mulberry, cherry and wild cherry, these woods being glued on both sides and held by bands made of cane or plaited bamboo bark.

So, by way of a number of metamorphoses, Japanese bows took on the definitive shape which they were to keep right up to the present day.

The bow in effect measures 8ft 10in (2.20m) long and is bent in the shape of a double curve. The grip from where the bow is drawn is positioned 28in (73cm) from the base, such that the tension occurs, as it were, a third of the way up the bow. The bow's great length, making it relatively difficult to

甲冑着用圖

Different types of Japanese armour. Top left (with sword): Momoyama and Edo periods; below (with nagamaki): infantry uniform, Kamakura and Muromachi periods; bottom left (with musket): infantry uniform, Momoyama and Edo periods; centre (two seated bowmen): Kamakura and beginning of the Muromachi periods; below (bowmen): Kamakura and Muromachi periods; to their right: uniform from the Heian and Kamakura periods; top right: Kamakura and Muromachi periods; below (two bowmen): Momoyama and Edo periods; bottom right: Kamakura and Muromachi periods.

handle in battle, is exclusive to the Japanese people. All other nations have adopted shorter and therefore more easily transportable varieties. These are usually drawn at the centre of the curve, whilst the Japanese bow is the only one which is held below the centre. The Japanese have always shown a particular form of reverence towards the bow, quite beyond its use in battle. One has to go back as far as the Assyrians to find this same veneration for the bow, for they considered it to be the most noble of all weapons. As for the Japanese, the Way of the sword and the Way of the bow rule supreme. There is a Japanese expression: 'the house of bow and arrows' which denotes a person's quality as a result of noble birth. The arrow which draws the bow is like the strength in man which can draw in the subtle power of the universe.

Finally, the bow and arrow were con-

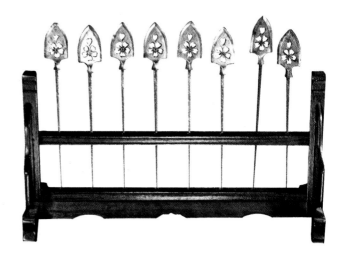

Arrow heads.

109

Bowmen on horseback.

sidered to be sacred by the Assyrians when they belonged to kings or generals.

In Shinto, the arrow is often an aid to purification. In fact, many temples have taken to selling arrows which are carried home and which, during the course of the year, absorb all things evil and impure. These arrows are then burnt during the end of year ceremonies. The manufacture of arrows itself has to follow a set of rules, which means the work always carries with it a deep significance.

Manufacture of the bow and arrow

The arrows are cut around the time of the winter solstice and left to dry for two to three months. It is very difficult to make a good arrow. In effect, one must know how to find the perfect bamboo cane and only one in two hundred can be used. It is necessary to choose a very straight bamboo cane and, as they all have knots, these must not be too prominent.

So, three-year-old canes are selected, the younger ones being too soft and older ones too hard. Nor must the arrows be too light or too heavy. If the bow is very powerful, the arrows must be tough and hard. If the bow is light, the arrows must of course be selected accordingly. The most difficult thing is to find arrows of the same quality at one time.

There once existed a type of arrow (kabu-ra-ya)[1] with a sort of ball on the tip, which gave off sounds intended to get rid of evil spirits when the arrow flew through the air. The size of the arrow is in itself beneficent or maleficent: if it is 2ft 8in (81cm) long, the arrow is beneficent. In fact, the figure itself is considered to be beneficent. According to Shinto interpretation, the figure 8 represents the circle. It is the sign of infinity, in other words the indeterminate number of things: 8, 888, 8888, etc.

The feathers (eagle or falcon) attached to the arrows also have a meaning. If white

[1] Kabura means 'turnip', hence arrow head in the shape of a turnip.

Bowmanship, sword practice and most of the martial arts inspired jugglers who performed unusual and extraordinary feats with the different weapons, a source of great public entertainment. This 17th century painting shows a juggler shooting an arrow with his feet.

feathers are chosen, it is because evil spirits are concealed in dark places and are frightened by white feathers; similarly, the bowstrings made from hemp and pine resin have particular qualities and make very special sounds.

The bow's draw-weight is considerable and measures from 33–88 lb (15–40 kg). It is generally the thickness of the bamboo surfaces and the different types of wood used which, in part, determine the draw-weight.

The arrow with the white eagle feathers is always used first. It measures from 38in (97.5cm) to 42in (1.1m) long, that is 1.2in (3cm) longer than all the other arrows. It is shot first as much to get rid of evil forces as to serve as a guide mark on the target. The other traditional arrows, four in all, are slightly shorter. They are also made of bamboo but scored with fine grooves. The four arrows, all alike, are grouped in pairs and must also be used in a certain order.

In traditional ceremonial archery, the five arrows are contained in a quiver made of cherry wood. The Japanese know that only the bamboo arrow can provide the sensory pleasure caused by the clearness of the noise made by the string when a shot occurs. Another characteristic of the bow: it is made in such a way that it is twice as light above the grip as it is below.

When in use, its asymmetrical length allows great beauty of movement; further-more, the Japanese bow is the only long bow which can be used on horseback. Because it is held at the shortest end, it can easily be passed over the horse's neck from one side to the other.

There are three different types of bowman-ship: standing, sitting and on horseback (yabusame).

The standing form includes two aspects (as in all the martial arts): *kyu-jitsu* or physical training in bowmanship, the object of which is to hit the target, and *shado* which is the spiritual training, the object of which is truth, goodness and beauty. The latter is primarily what Master Anzawa used to teach.

Ceremonial bowmanship performed by Master Nakano. Note the sword carrier in the background.

Concentration prior to shooting. Hideharu Onuma, a follower of Master Anzawa.

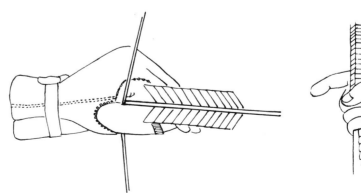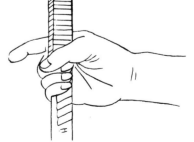

Diagrams: method of holding the bow, the end of the arrow and aiming the bow at the target.

Every year, a competition is held in the great Buddhist temple: the Sanjusangendo, in Kyoto. The contest has existed since 1606. It involves shooting the greatest possible number of arrows at the target in one day. The record is still held by Wasa Daichiro who in 1696 is said to have fired 13,053 arrows of which 8,133 hit the target. The bowman shoots from south to north. His shooting angle is limited on his right by the porch roof and the temple's outside gallery. Here, Master Kitajima is seen taking part in the Sanjusangendo competition.

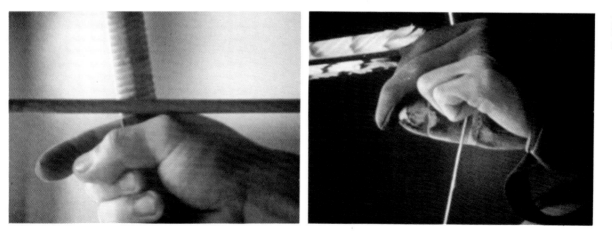

Method of holding the bow and gripping the string.

115

GROUP KYUDO

The dojo is a sort of room raised above ground level and open at the front. The wooden floor must always be kept meticulously clean and shining. The target is situated 65yds (60m) away, facing the dojo. The action resembles a sort of choreography with very slow movements.

The Japanese bow is long and asymmetrical. The draw-weight of the string varies from 33–88 lb (15–40 kg). Only the very great masters are able to draw the powerful bows. The strength of the arrow is of course proportional to the draw-weight of the bow and the strength of the bow relative to its thickness.

(a) Yazuka.

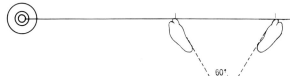

(b) Angle of the feet in relation to the target's axis: 60°; also distance between the feet corresponding to the length of the arrow.

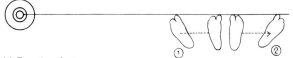

(c) Practice shot.

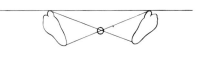

(d) Position of the centre of the body in relation to the feet.

1. ASHIBUMI: positioning of the feet

(a) Yazuka: the way of determining the appropriate length of an arrow.
(b) Angle of the feet in relation to the target's axis and also distance between the feet, corresponding to the length of the arrow.
(c) Practice shot.
(d) Position of the centre of the body in relation to the feet.
(e) Ashibumi-no-kata: positioning of the feet and position of the bow and arrow in relation to the line of posture.
The distance between the feet corresponds to the length of the arrow.

2. DOZUKURI: steadying the body

The bowman straightens his spine, fixes his centre of gravity and adjusts his breathing.
(a) Line of strength in the legs: the strength is concentrated on the inside of the legs.
(b) The other lines (the axial line and the parallels) relate to posture.
(c) Position of the bow in relation to the line of posture.
(d) Line of the shoulders.
(e) Line of the hips, parallel to each other.

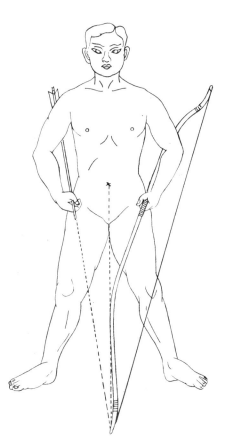

1. **ASHIBUMI: positioning of the feet.**

2. **DOZUKURI: steadying the body.**

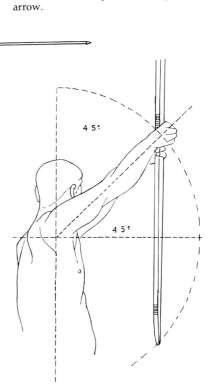

The line of vision is parallel to the path of the arrow.

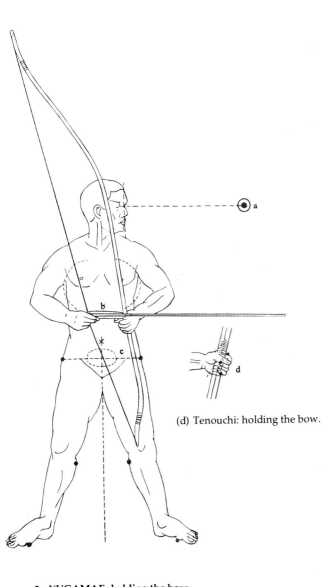

(d) Tenouchi: holding the bow.

3. YUGAMAE: holding the bow

The bowman prepares to shoot; he attaches his glove and checks his tenouchi (hold on the bow).
(a) Head perpendicular to the target's axis.
(b) Arms spaced as though embracing a tree.
(c) Concentration of energy in the hara.
(d) Tenouchi: holding the bow.

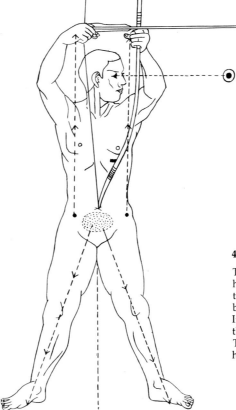

The bowman is imagined to be in the centre of a semi-circle.
The raising of the arm inscribes an angle of 45° in the middle.

4. UCHIOKOSHI: raising the bow

The bowman raises the bow at arms' length; he does not raise his shoulders at the same time but lowers them. He steadies his breathing.
In the lower part of the body, the strength of the hara goes into the axes of the legs.
The raising of the bow is an action from the hips.

119

5. HIKIWAKE: drawing the bow in stages

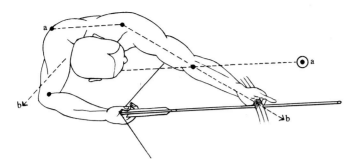

(a) Lines of posture.
(b) Lines of strength. It can be seen that the action of extending the bow goes from the shoulder to infinity, whilst the pull on the string goes outwards from the elbow.

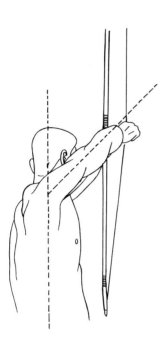

Lines of posture and angle of the arm in relation to posture.

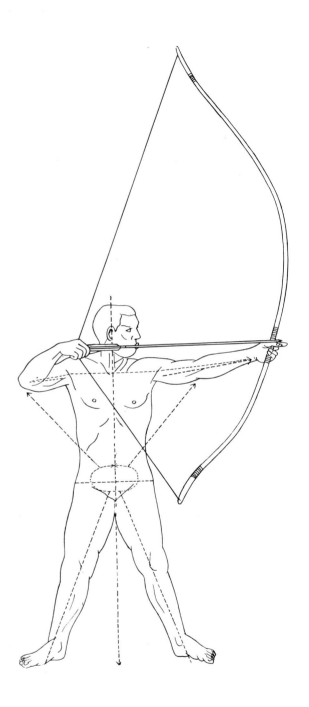

5. HIKIWAKE: drawing the bow in stages

Drawing the bow consists of two stages:
(a) Daisan: the Great Third.
The archer pushes the bow away from him with his left hand, along a third of the arrow's length, holding the string back with his right hand.
(b) Hikiwake: action of completing the draw.

6. KAI: the Union

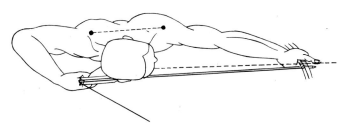

Kai or the Union (seen from above). Note that ideally the position of the shoulders is parallel with the sight line to the target.

THE EIGHT POSITIONS AND RULES OF BOWMANSHIP

1. **Positioning of the feet** — ashibumi
2. **Steadying the body** — dozukuri
3. **Holding the bow** — yugamae
4. **Raising the bow** — uchiokoshi
5. **Drawing the bow in stages** — hikiwake
6. **The Union** — kai
7. **The Loose** — hanare
8. **Follow-through** — zanshin

Positions taken from the diagrams of the Zen Nippon Kyudo Renmei.

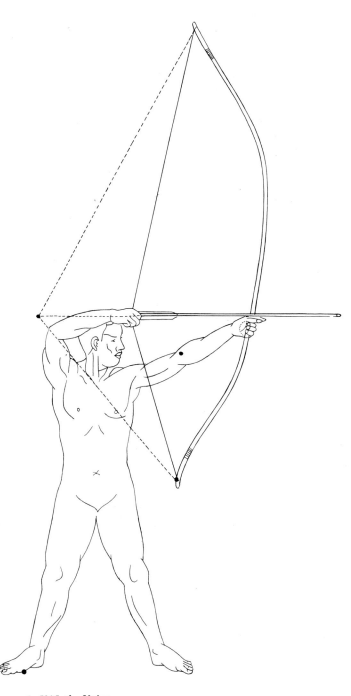

7. HANARE: the Loose

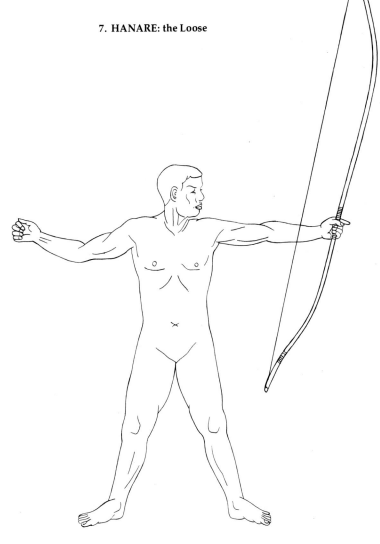

6. KAI: the Union

Hikiwake ends when the bow is fully drawn: it is the moment of union of mind and body and of distribution of energy to different parts of the body.

7. HANARE: the Loose

When the time is 'ripe', the arrow flies, as a fruit falls from a tree.

8. ZANSHIN: follow-through

The arrow has gone but the shot continues. Same position as 7. Zanshin is an attitude of mind.

Herrigel and Master Awa's teaching

In 1923, a German professor of philosophy named Herrigel arrived in Tokyo. After three years spent in learning about Japanese thought, Zen in particular, he met the great master of kyudo: Awa. Under his guidance, Herrigel spent five years learning what he later called *Zen in the Chivalrous Art of Bowmanship,* the title of a small indispensable book describing this experience.[1]

The instruction begins by shooting at the makiwara, a sort of straw bundle on which the novice practises shooting arrows. He learns how to position his feet, draw the bow, control his breathing and his stomach muscles.

The master would take hold of Herrigel's bow and guide his arm in practice, then step back. Herrigel would now be standing with the bow drawn, awaiting the order to shoot. 'Not yet', the master would say and Herrigel would begin to tremble with the effort required of him. 'Not yet', the master would say again, slapping Herrigel's stomach with the palm of his hand. 'Try harder! Stretch your stomach muscles!' he would cry and when the bow was fully drawn: 'Breath out fully but do not breath in and do not shoot yet.' From time to time the master would come up and put his ear against his pupil's nose to check he was not breathing in, and would then slap his stomach and repeat 'Not yet, not yet! Patience! Hold on!'

Herrigel would finish the exercise completely exhausted. 'As long as you insist on

[1] Published (in French) by Dervy-Livres, Paris.

The great Master Anzawa standing in his garden before shooting.

Master Kazuo Suhara.

Master Kazuo Suhara is one of the Superiors of the great Zen temple, Engakuji, near Kamakura. Like all the great masters of bowmanship, Master Suhara never explains what he knows. Skill in shooting is above all the practice of shooting. The movements are painfully slow. It is the point of concentration which releases the arrow. The shot is only pure if one's will plays no part in it. For the truly initiated, the target is always of secondary importance.

This extraordinary picture records the face of Master Anzawa at the precise moment when, pulling back the arrow, he has just uttered the kiai. The tension and gravity in his face reflect the intensity and the concentration put into the shot.

using your strength, you can do nothing', the master would say. 'To shoot well, you must forget your physical strength and shoot only with your strength of mind.'

It took more than a year's training before Herrigel had mastered the tanden (control over the abdomen and breathing) and could shoot without calling on his physical strength.

Every time the pupil made some progress, the master would let him shoot at the proper target. 'Never think of the target when you shoot the arrow', the master would say. 'It is a banal action to shoot at the target a hundred times, but if you do shoot a hundred times, it is a sacred action to complete a hundred perfect shots.' And again: 'To shoot at the target is no different to shooting at one's self.'

Herrigel left Sendai Imperial University in August 1929 to return to Germany. He was a new man. Apart from the bow, Master Awa had made him discover the unity of a teaching which was also a unity of life: not the skilful execution of the shot but the opposite, a self-control over both mind and techniques, like deep natural breathing.

QUALITY OF THE SHOT

1. Coordinated actions and disorderly actions.
2. The controlled shot and the careless shot.
3. The shot which never stands still and the dull shot.
4. The shot from the stomach and the shot from the upper part of the body.
5. The shot with logical breathing and the shot with forced breathing.
6. The over-cautious shot and the thoughtless, hasty shot.
7. The magnificent shot and the dextrous shot.
8. The light shot and the dark shot.
9. The honest and dishonest shot.
10. The trained shot and the untrained shot.
11. Suppleness and rigidity.
12. The shot by correct positioning and the shot using incorrect movements.
13. The shot with clear vision and the shot lacking perspicacity.
14. The uniform shot and the disorderly shot.
15. The shot from the soul and the shot caused by strength.
16. The profound shot and the superficial shot.
17. The transcendant shot and the premeditated shot.
18. The spontaneous shot and the shot aimed.
19. The good shot and the impure shot.
20. The anticipated shot and the unexpected shot.
21. The solemn shot and the vulgar shot.
22. The shot without self-interest, and the self-centred shot.
23. The shot effected by the strength of the stomach and the one effected by the strength of the head.
24. The 'ripe' shot without propulsion and the shot effected with false strength.

The thoughts of Master Anzawa

The shot must enhance a form which is wise and profound, great and supreme. The natural expression of oneself in kyudo must be the accomplishment of the unity of the three principles: 'Truth, Goodness and Beauty'.

Basic principle: one life, one shot. Spend your whole lifetime shooting one arrow.

The skill is learnt without speech.

If you want to live in harmony with heaven and earth, which is the way of kyudo, do not try to attain the goal. Do not seek the pleasure of reaching the goal; take the path which unites body and soul.

The true form of the shot lies in the identification of the conscience and the act of shooting.

All training lacking in the spirit of the Way can include violence. The shot with no Way is always a mediocre and degenerate shot.

The 'true self', that is to say the authentic self, is divinity, Buddheity, or the profound ego (according to which term you prefer) but it is above all the immortal soul which has its place in the stomach (tanden). This pure soul which exists in the tanden works effectively and is the very thing that must be called the 'true self'.

The disciples of shado who want to live in this supreme and noble Way must never for a moment forget the great spirit of spontaneity, of self-abandon, which enables one to enter the sacred world of the Absolute, of the non-ego, and there to achieve supreme beauty.

So, it is necessary to define the fundamental difference between the Way of bowmanship: kyudo or shado, and the technique: kyujutsu. Kyudo or shado is a means of putting oneself to the test by the relationship which exists between oneself and the target, whilst kyujutsu, from feudal times, principally means the handling of the weapon with a view to murdering the enemy.

THE 'PRESENCE OF MIND' OR THE POWER TO SHOOT,
by Master Awa

'Remember that the object of bowmanship is not to strengthen one's muscles. In drawing the string, one must not use the full strength of the body, but learn to let both hands carry out the work, while the muscles in the arms and shoulders stay relaxed and appear not to be playing any part in the action. Only when you can do that will you have fulfilled just one of the conditions which will enable you to bend a bow and shoot in spirit.

'Act as though the goal was infinity. For us, masters of the bow, this is a known fact confirmed by daily experience. A good bowman shoots further with a bow of medium power than a soulless bowman with the most powerful bow. The result is not due to the bow but to the ''presence of mind'', to the vitality and the state of alertness with which you shoot.

'You must hold the taut string as a child holds a finger offered to him. He grips it so tightly that one never ceases to wonder at the strength of such a tiny wrist. And, when he lets go of the finger, he does it without the slightest jerk. Do you know why? Because the child does not think for example: ''I am going to drop this finger in order to take hold of this other thing.'' Rather, it is without a thought and without his knowledge that he goes from one thing to another, and one would say that he was playing with things, were it not equally true to think that the things were playing with him.

'True art has no goal and no purpose. Obstinately, you will persevere in wishing to learn to release the arrow, no doubt in order to achieve an objective, but the more you succeed, the further the goal recedes from you.'

Quotations from Herrigel's work: *Zen in the Chivalrous Art of Bowmanship,* Dervy-Livres, Paris.

Master Awa (1880-1939). Great master of kyudo whose most famous disciples were: Master Anzawa (1887-1970) and Eugen Herrigel. This photograph is a very rare document. It shows the master executing a Reisha, a ceremonial or noble shooting in which the master bares his left shoulder.

Professor Herrigel was the first European to penetrate the mysterious world of Japanese bowmanship. He was awarded the 5th Dan, the highest distinction ever acquired by a non-Japanese.

The three masters (right to left) Onuma, Kitajima and Suhara, in the zazen position prior to shooting. Note behind them the two makiwara or straw bundles used in training.

Bowmanship expressed in Zen and Shinto terms

So, the practice of archery is above all an exercise of serenity and spiritual discipline. 'True art', said Master Awa, 'has no goal and no purpose. The greater one's desire to attain an objective, the less likely one is to do so. One's will, intent on a result, is the obstacle. We also say: "With one end of his bow the bowman pierces the sky, at the other end is the earth, attached to a silk thread." If the shot is released with a sudden jolt, one is exposed to the danger of seeing the thread break. Man rests between sky and earth in this intermediate position which offers no refuge.'

In Japan, many people are devotees of traditional bowmanship: (between 450,000 and 500,000). There are various associations of kyudo, all united under the aegis of the Japanese Kyudo Federation, and even a grand competition which takes place on 15 January each year in the great hall of Sanjusangendo, a Buddhist temple in Kyoto. The archer who shoots the greatest number of arrows from one end of the hall to the other, about 142yds (130m), is declared the winner. The record is still held by Wasa Daichiro, a samurai (see page 115).

Kyudo is nevertheless one of the martial arts which attracts a high class of followers. Many university professors, research workers, artists and writers, practise kyudo. It is a long and difficult art which requires total self-abandon and unreserved confidence in the master. Only he can discover what is the driving force in the pupil.

Ceremonial kyudo by Master Nakano.

Master Nakano (10th Hanshi Dan), the greatest living master in Japan today, concentrates before the shot.

The ceremonial shot has a Shinto significance. The arrow is weighted with a device shaped like a turnip which produces sounds as it travels through the air. These sounds are to frighten off the evil spirits.

During the ceremony the great master is assisted by an attendant, a sword bearer and a bow carrier.

Shinto kyudo ceremony outside the Meiji temple in Tokyo, conducted by the great priest Yamakage.

Kyudo is also a religious expression. The Shinto religion celebrates the spirit of the arrow which alone can cross the world, pierce the heart of the cosmos, unite the visible and the invisible.

129

庄子市

Samurai bowmen have at all times been famous for their accomplished skill.
Here, the whole art is in the breathing: synchronizing the shot with the breathing, the moving with the stationary; that, people say, is the secret of success.

Bowmanship on horseback or yabusame

Bowmanship on horseback is one of the first skills of the samurai.

Shooting on horseback could also have a symbolic and religious significance in the Shinto rite.

In the 17th century, at the start of the Tokugawa era, bowmanship lost its military value with the introduction of fire arms. However, in the middle of the last century, during the Meiji era, Yabusame became popular once more and rediscovered its religious significance. Now, every year, on 15 and 16 September, the festival and the ceremony of archery are celebrated in the Hachiman Shinto temple in Kamakura.

Adorned in a magnificent 15th-century costume, the great Master Kaneko Yurin officiates at the ceremony. Right at the beginning, a kannuchi or Shinto priest gives his blessing. Three targets are positioned on the course which is 238yds (218m) long and cordoned off. The preparation for this moment has been extremely thorough. For the master and riders alike, the few seconds when they will send three arrows flying into the targets at a full gallop are the result of a whole year's preparation. The good health of the horse and rider, the perfect state of the bow and arrows, the harness, the smallest details have all received constant attention.

This ceremony is principally a hommage to the emperor. That is why Master Kaneko holds an arrow up towards heaven and then down to earth (tenchi) as a sign of unity and to call for the prosperity and the protection of the imperial family. All the rites in yabusame, even down to the least significant – for example drinking a cup full of sake after the shooting – incorporate the same idea linking man to the cosmic powers.

Before running to string his bow and shoot 100yds. further on, the rider concentrates. The secret of success is to harmonize one's breathing with the shot and the moving object with the stationary one.

Master Kaneko Yurin at home. His house near Kamakura is a veritable museum of chivalry. He has put beside him the essential items of equipment (saddle, stirrups, hat, sword and bow) which are necessary for the Shinto yabusame ceremony.

The Way of the sword

Iizasa Morisada

The scene is set in the 19th century. A band of samurai quietly surround an inn. They are the men of the last shogun (Japanese military dictator). Inside the tavern, more samurai conspire against him. Japan is in a state of crisis; the emperor who has been powerless for centuries, is the only one who can bring about the unity of the Japanese people against threats from the West. Leading the conspirators is one Iizasa Morisada.

Suddenly, the shogun's troops invade the room, brandishing their swords. With his sword, Morisada executes a striking action in the direction of the candle facing him inside a lantern made of wood and paper, giving off a dim light. Morisada then lifts up the top of the lantern showing that he has cut both the candle and the lantern in two without letting them fall.

His enemies are so stupefied and frightened that they flee.

Master Otake is just as painstaking with the religious tradition of his ryu. All training sessions are preceded by a visit to the Sanctuary where, together with his pupils, he receives purification according to Shinto religious rites.

These signs complete a collection of nine which constitute the signs of concentration. They are only taught to the initiates.

Master Otake says: 'One must be able to summon concentration at any time and in any place.'

Penitence and rules of combat

Such impressive acts are numerous and legendary in samurai history. As for Morisada, he belonged to one of Japan's most famous ryu: The Katori Shinto Ryu, created by Izasa Choisai (1387-1488). He was a brave samurai who practised Shinto.

One day, while he was in the Kashima and Katori sanctuary dedicated to Futsu Nushi, a kami of war, Choisai had the idea of washing his horse's feet in the temple fountain. Immediately, the horse fell down dead.

Izasa understood that he had just committed a sacrilege. The water at the sanctuary was reserved for the sole purpose of purifying the faithful. As a sign of penitence, he shut himself in the temple for a thousand days, devoting his time to meditation and the art of the sword.

So, he had plenty of time to perfect new rules of combat out of which grew the Tenshin Shoden Katori Shinto Ryu, known as the Katori ryu, which he founded when his penitence was over.

Ever since, the tradition has been handed down from father to son. Today, the heir to the dynasty, Yasusada, as yet too young and inexperienced, is trained by Master Otake who at present runs the ryu. His followers number about 1000 throughout Japan and his initiates fewer than about 30.

The handing down of the secrets is in actual fact extremely strict. The initiate must sign with his blood (a slight prick of the finger) as a pledge that he will never disclose anything he has learnt. 'That too is a secret', Master Otake would say, smiling.

The instruction lasts many years. During the first three, the pupil must practise the exercises and at the end of this time receives the first diploma. Then, three or four years later, a second parchment and finally, those who are able to attain a certain level are entitled to initiation instruction, of which the nine signs necessary for concentration are a part.

Meditation is done in the zazen position. As for the spiritual teaching, one phrase sums it up: 'Once you start a fight, you must win', says Master Otake, 'but fighting is not the object. The art of war is the art of peace; the art of peace is the most difficult: you must win without fighting.'

Attack with the sword and defense with the sai, by Master Shiokawa.

The life of Miyamoto Musashi

There is no story and no life more famous amongst the samurai than that of Miyamoto Musashi (1584-1645) – and rightly so, for Musashi added a unique dimension to the image of the great samurai master.

It seems he was born with the gift of the sword because his fame developed at an early age. At 13 he fought and killed Master Arima of the Shinto-Ryu.

It is likely that his father, Munisai

Shinmen, the reputable master of swordsmanship, taught him the art of the sword. But this alone would not have been sufficient to explain either his precociousness or his extraordinary virtuosity. In 61 years of life, he entered into about 66 fights, often against a large number of opponents at a time and remained unconquered. [1]

During a sword contest, Musashi's father, Munisai, challenged a young samurai who was acknowledged to be a great master, Ganryu Sasaki, and defeated him. Sasaki, humiliated, later murdered Munisai by deceiving him.

Miyamoto Musashi set about looking for him, found him and the two young masters engaged in a memorable fight from which Musashi emerged as the winner.

Musashi's biography seems to consist of a series of spectacular fights. Yet, at the age of 30, he seemed tired of this lifestyle. He was, in fact, a man of great delicacy and culture. He practised calligraphy in which he excelled, as well as classical painting, was interested in poetry and above all exercised his mind in meditation. He worked continuously at his special sword technique, imagining it was far from perfect.

Following some intense periods of meditation, Musashi became aware of an extraordinary inward experience: the awakening which opened 'the Way of life'. After this experience, he created his famous Enmei ryu of the two swords which later became the Niten-Ichi-Ryu.

His technique recommended holding the long sword (or daito) in the right hand and a short sword in the left. In two sword combats, the long one was used first in a slicing motion and the short one served to deliver a whiplash or lunge.

At the age of 60, Musashi retired into a cave where he chose to live in great poverty. This enabled him to write *Essays on the Five Circles* (*Gorin no Sho*), which he completed two years later in May 1645.

As well as being a spiritual testament, this work gives instruction in sword tactics, which however could not be very easily understood by other than a trained student. This manuscript was never intended for circulation but according to custom, the master left it to his successor, Terao Katsunobu, so that he in his turn could hand it down and so on, from generation to generation.

---

[1] With the exception of the famous fight against Master Muso described further on.

Musashi died on 19 May 1645. His tomb near the town of Kumamoto is today still a place of pilgrimage.

Earth, water, fire, wind and Void

Musashi's exceptional greatness undeniably contributed to the importance of his teaching.

Firstly, he did not refrain from criticizing the people of his time, with repercussions similar to those which are commonplace today.

'If I look around me', he said, 'I conclude that everyone treats art as commerce, that men themselves are regarded as merchandise, that objects are only made in order to be sold. . .

'. . . People in other schools use their tactics to earn their living and thus convey an outward appearance of glamour, embellishing it and commercializing it; therefore they are completely removed from the true Way.

'For these people, tactics are confined to swordsmanship and they wish to achieve victory simply by knowing how to handle a sword, how to control the body and by sleight of hand; but these are not the sure ways.'

That extract was written in the fifth chapter which he called 'Wind' and which is devoted to criticism of the different ryu.

'When I observe the tactics of other ryu, I can tell which of them use the large sword and employ muscular strength exclusively. Others are only concerned with the restrictive sword technique and even divide the care of the sword into the superficial and the profound. . .'

Musashi's subtle teaching has already been outlined in the previous chapter entitled 'The Spirit of Budo'; however, by way of complementing it, we will quote Musashi's own words:

'Practise morning and evening according to the Way of tactics of our ryu, as described above. So, your ideas will expand and my tactics will, in an adapted form, be made known to crowds of people or to one alone. For the first time, I am putting my thoughts on paper and this will comprise five chapters: Earth, Water, Fire, Wind and Void. . .

'. . . The important thing is that, within this Way, you cannot become an expert in tactics unless you have a direct and broad attitude. If you possess such an ability, you alone could not be beaten by 20 or 30 adversaries at once. First, one must always bear the tactics in mind and practise relentlessly and then we will conquer others with our own hands and *your*

Kabuki actor miming a samurai. Print by Toyokuni, Edo period.

attitude will be superior to that of others. And if your whole body is liberated through practice, then you will be superior to others by virtue of your own body. And if your mind is fully accustomed to the Way, you can conquer others by virtue of your own mind. If you reach this point, how can you possibly be beaten by others?

'So, in the field of tactics applied to a crowd, you will win in order to retain the good men, you will win in order to make use of many men, you will win in order that your conduct is always good, you will win in order to govern the country, you will win in order to feed the people and you will win with a view to maintaining order in the world. Thus, in all fields, you will know how to avoid being beaten by others. And finally, you will help yourself and your honour: that is the Way of tactics.'

The Japanese sword

In the latter part of the Kamakura era (1192-1333) there were two great swordsmiths named Masamune and Muramasa.

Goro Masamune, whose works are today considered to be the finest in the country, never forged a sword without first offering up prayers and undergoing the customary purification rites. He surrounded his workshop with holy ropes and, in ceremonial dress, he asked for the protection of the good spirits.

Whilst forging the blade itself, Masamune maintained a religious intensity and concentration: the blade became the product of this mental, physical and spiritual power.

Muramasa, on the other hand, was a master smith who liked war. He was just as skilled as Masamune but withdrawn and subdued in character. His swords which were robust when put to any test, were much sought after: it was said that they could cut through tough iron helmets like melons. Yet, owners of these swords wanted to get rid of them as they had the reputation of being evil, blood-thirsty swords. Some of their owners, it is said, went mad, killing many people before committing suicide themselves.

Legend says that, to tell the difference between one of Masamune's blades and one of Muramasa's, all you had to do was to place the two swords in the running water of a stream. In effect, the dead leaves flowing downstream avoided Masamune's blade, whilst they were attracted to that of Muramasa and were cut in half. This story dealing with the maleficent and beneficent effects of swords is just one of many in Japan.

It is obvious that such a determinant relationship between man and his sword creates a considerable psychological strength in terms of identity. Oriental custom in some cases involved 'charging the objects of life' or in other words adding a sort of supporting magic to them: sword, statue, object, etc., is the effect of a tradition so old and so subtle that it would be absurd to evaluate it from the point of view of our rational and sceptical culture. The sword revealed the samurai's personality to such an extent that Toyotomi Hideyoshi by examining a blade could tell to which of his generals it belonged.

The Japanese sword has always been an object of profound veneration, ever since it was made by a known and highly regarded master. The life of the sword was sometimes preserved, whatever the outcome of battle, as it stood for personal wealth (often all that an old samurai, turned ronin, had left), family heritage (ceremoniously handed down from father to son), and national heritage.

In Japan there are about 900,000 katana of all kinds catalogued in museums, sanctuaries, temples and private collections, throughout the country. Many of these weapons are classified as 'national treasures' or 'important objects of culture' and worth fortunes.

The manufacture of the Japanese sword has in fact throughout the centuries attained an exceptional degree of perfection. It is founded on the traditional elements: iron, fire, clay, water and wood, as well as man. The sword rises from the combination and the quality of these six elements. That is why every sword is unique and why by this very fact, the armourer is himself incapable of producing two the same.

Even today, there are some great masters in Japan who forge 12 or 13 swords a year on average. Although the actual manufacture of the sword only takes about two weeks as a rule, several months, even a year, elapse between the order and the delivery. The master armourer in fact requires a long period of reflection to decide on the model he is to forge. For a master, sword making is above all the expression of an inward harmony: the time, the hour, the positions of the planets, all play their part. Before setting to work, the master armourer carries out ablutions using pure cold water to ward off evil influences. He covers his head in black and wears spotless white clothes as a symbol of purity. These rites together lend a sort of sacredness to the making of the sword. It becomes an object with a personality of its own, having a 'soul'; and is therefore handled with the greatest respect.

We must remember that the three sacred treasures of Japan are the sword, the jewel (or tama) and the mirror. The sword plays a prominent part in Japanese mythology, folklore and history.

Susa no wo no mikoto, son of Izanagi and nephew of the Sun Goddess Amaterasu, slew the eight-headed dragon and in its tail found the sword which became one of the three sacred treasures.

This sword (named Ama no Murakumo no Tsurugi) was kept in the Ise temple. When a revolt occurred in the Suruga province, it was entrusted to the son of Emperor Keiko (in 70, 130 AD) to quell the rebellion. According to a legend, the emperor's son surrounded by fire in a burning meadow, was saved by his sword which sprung out of the scabbard and cut down all the grass around him, providing an exit. This blade was then rebaptized 'grass cutter'.

Susa no wo, an unruly kami expelled from the celestial paradise, came down to earth to kill a mighty dragon. In its tail, Susa no wo found a long sword which, together with the mirror and the magatama or sacred jewel, became one of the three symbols of the emperor. (From a reenactment of the scene given at the Izumo Sanctuary.)

Manufacture and beauty of the sword

The beauty of a katana is the result of four qualities: its shape, the lie of the grain on the blade, the undulating pattern on the cutting edge and the minute dots which make up the design along the edge.

The oldest swords are also the most in demand. Until the 16th century, steel was made from iron melted down with charcoal worked into cavities made on the side of the blade exposed to the beating. The steel with a low carbon content stayed exceptionally supple. After the 16th century, the use of bellows which raised the temperature of the ovens produced an alloy with a higher carbon content.

The metal obtained is then hammered until a thin sheet of steel is obtained. After being hammered and worked day after day, this sheet of steel is used to cover the body of the sword, made of a softer metal. The combination of the hard and soft metals gives the blade its flexibility and its strength.

Once the sword has taken on its shape, the process of retempering begins. A clay-based compound is applied thinly to the cutting edge and generously to the rest of the sword. The undulating pattern on the cutting edge depends on the way in which this mixture is applied. For the most part, this process is a professional secret and often enables one to recognize the craftsman's skill. The difference in thickness of the clay between the cutting edge and the rib gives a blade with a varying grain, the more tempered part being called *nie* and the rib *nioi*. Nie suggests spirit, a virile nature; nioi signifies dignity and nobility. The synthesis between the nie and the nioi is an important criterion in evaluating a katana.

The final stage of the work consists of sharpening and polishing. This can only be done by experienced masters because the cutting edge and the beauty and richness of the blade's decoration depend on it. One can understand why at the end of the war the Japanese went to all lengths to recover or buy back all the swords of value taken by the Americans or in the hands of collectors throughout the world. In 1965, the Museum of Japanese Swords was founded in Sukiyabashi, Tokyo. There is also a Japanese Society for conserving swords of beauty (Nippon Bijutsu Token Honzon Kyokai).

JAPANESE SWORDS

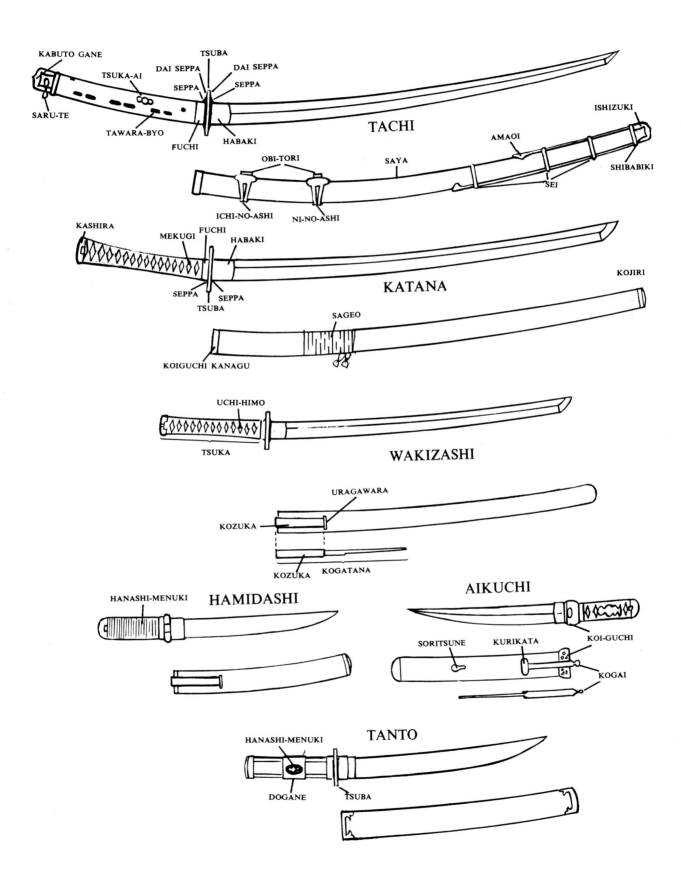

KABUTO GANE
TSUBA
TSUKA-AI
DAI SEPPA
DAI SEPPA
SEPPA
SEPPA
SARU-TE
TAWARA-BYO
FUCHI
HABAKI
TACHI
ISHIZUKI
AMAOI
SHIBABIKI
OBI-TORI
SAYA
SEI
ICHI-NO-ASHI
NI-NO-ASHI

KASHIRA
MEKUGI
FUCHI
HABAKI
KOJIRI
KATANA
SEPPA
SEPPA
TSUBA
SAGEO
KOIGUCHI KANAGU

UCHI-HIMO
TSUKA
WAKIZASHI

URAGAWARA
KOZUKA
KOZUKA
KOGATANA

HANASHI-MENUKI
HAMIDASHI
AIKUCHI
SORITSUNE
KURIKATA
KOI-GUCHI
KOGAI

HANASHI-MENUKI
TANTO
DOGANE
TSUBA

Iai

Iai or the art of drawing the sword

A samurai only ever sleeps with one eye shut: custom has taught him to lie in such a way that whatever happens he can leap up at the slightest alarm, his sword in his hand. Similarly, a samurai only ever drinks tea with his left hand and resting on one knee – the right one – with his left leg raised and ready to leap whilst the right hand will make the sword spring out of the scabbard (saya). In Japan, to draw the sword in one almost instantaneous action, in addition to being an art form of remarkable formal beauty, became an absolute necessity, as in the event of an attack, life could depend on a fraction of a second.

The art of drawing the sword or iaijutsu developed around the 15th century. The Muso-Ryu was, it seems, the first to introduce iai, followed in time by 412 ryu, all of which employed highly secret methods, learning to draw the sword and to defend themselves whilst standing, lying, sitting, kneeling, etc.

After the Tokugawa era, iaijutsu lost its offensive nature and became established as a technique used by all the samurai and implying serenity of spirit, control of respiration and, above all, the sign of perfect and elegant self-control in the art of drawing the sword.

During the Meiji era, different forms of iaido emerged, in spite of opposition from the old ryu, which even today perform traditional styles of iaijutsu. In iaido (nowadays controlled by the Japanese Kendo Federation), the actions required to draw the sword are limited to 20 and the figures in cutting to 50.

It is seldom that a reunion of masters of the martial arts ends without a iai demonstration. The practice of iaido is symbolic of perfection itself in budo.

Master Noda from the Katori Shinto Ryu.

Like all the old masters of the martial arts, Master Noda, aged 82, performs iai, or the art of drawing the sword. In fact, iai is an introduction to all the martial arts. It is taught in several schools but only the one which displays absolute perfection is worthy of the title of grand master.

Today, several schools such as the Katori keep alive the tradition of iaijutsu, in other words an extremely swift process, which literally causes the blade to spring out of the scabbard. The modern version of iai is called iaido, its prime purpose being to teach the art of breathing and serenity of spirit.

Iai by Master Kuroda Ichitaro

Five figures in iai by Master Kuroda Ichitaro, 7th Dan, in the garden of the Meiji temple in Tokyo.

1. Resting with weight on the left heel.
2. Draw and attack the enemy at the knees.
3. Prepare to cut vertically through the enemy's head.
4. This done – pause a moment, without loss of concentration: zenshin.
5. Turn the sword to let the blood flow: chiburi.
6. Prepare to replace the sword in its sheath.

1	2	3
4	5	6

Tameshi-giri

Tameshi-giri: the art of cutting

The curious art of tameshi-giri or the art of cutting with a sword, was at all times practised in Japan.

To test their sword blades, the samurai used their skill to cut up the bodies and limbs of convicts. Once there were tameshi-giri professionals, men of great ability, who practised the cutting movement several hundred times a day.

Today, masters and pupils practise on columns of damp straw or bamboo stakes. Here Master Nakamura Taizaburo demonstrates four examples of the art.

THREE SAMURAI STORIES

The four flies

A samurai was calmly eating his supper in a small inn, ignoring four flies which kept buzzing round him. Three ronin (masterless samurai) came in: they looked enviously at the two magnificent swords which the man had fixed in his belt, for these weapons represented a small fortune. A look of intense satisfaction came over their faces: the man seemed to be defenceless and alone against three.

Sitting at a nearby table, they began to make fun of him in raised voices in the hope that he would be provoked into a duel. As the man remained completely indifferent to them, they got more and more acid. So, slowly raising the chopsticks with which he had just eaten his rice, the samurai effortlessly struck each of the four flies in four quick, precise actions, after which he delicately put down the tools, and all without so much as glancing at the three boors. A heavy silence followed. The three ronin looking at each other realized that before them was a man of formidable mastery. Frightened, they fled.

Much later, they learnt that this man who had so shrewdly spared them was called Miyamoto Musashi . . .

The master and his three sons

There was once a great master of kenjutsu (sword) renowned throughout Japan who, when visited by another great master, wished to demonstrate the teaching he had given his three sons.

The master winked at his guest and placed a heavy metal vase on the corner of the sliding doors, wedged it with a piece of bamboo and a small nail in such a way that the vase would fall on the head of the first one who came into the room when the door was opened.

While chatting and drinking tea, the master called his oldest son who came immediately. Before opening the door, he felt the presence of the vase and its position. He slid back the door, put his left hand through the gap to catch the vase and continued opening the door with his right hand. Then, clutching the vase to his chest, he entered the room, shutting the door behind him and replaced the vase; he came forward and greeted the two masters. 'This is my oldest son', said the host smiling, 'he has learnt my teaching well and one day he will undoubtedly be a master of kenjutsu.'

The second son was called and he entered without hesitating and only caught the vase at the last moment: it almost landed on his head. 'This is my second son', said the master, 'he still has a lot to learn but he is improving every day.'

Then the third son was called. Entering the room hurriedly, he was struck on the head by the vase. The blow was a heavy one but before the vase hit the tatami, he drew his sword and, in one quick action, cut the piece of metal in two. 'This is my youngest son, Jiro', said the old man, 'he is the baby of the family and he still has a long way to go.'

The tea master and the ronin

A master of chado (the Way of the tea ceremony), Tajima Kozo, was challenged to a duel by an unscrupulous ronin who was confident of winning with ease. As he could not refuse the challenge without loss of honour, the master prepared to die.

He therefore went to call on a neighbouring master of kenjutsu and asked him to teach him how to die properly. 'Your intention is most laudable', said the expert 'and I should be very happy to help you, but first of all kindly serve me a cup of tea please.' Tajima was delighted to have the chance to practise his skill, probably for the last time, and so he was totally absorbed in the ceremony of preparing the tea, forgetting what was in store for him. The expert was deeply impressed by his degree of serenity at such a solemn time: 'There is no need for me to teach you how to die', he told him. 'Your concentration of mind is so great that you can let yourself encounter any sword expert. When you are facing the ronin, first imagine that you are about to serve tea to a guest. Greet him courteously. Take off your coat, fold it carefully and place your fan on top of it, exactly as you have just done. Then draw your katana and raise it above your head, ready to strike when the opponent attacks, and concentrate on this action alone.'

Tajima thanked him and went to the place appointed for the fight. He followed the expert's advice and totally absorbed himself with the thought that he was about to serve tea to a friend. When he raised his sword above his head, the ronin sensed that before him was an entirely different character; he could see no way round him; Tajima seemed to him as solid as a rock, completely without fear or weakness.

So the ronin, demoralized by this behaviour, threw down his katana and prostrating himself before Tajima, humbly asked forgiveness for his unspeakable conduct.

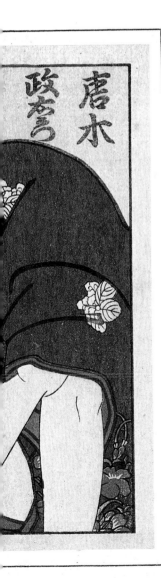

Bowman, Maniwa-Nen ryu. To learn to draw the sword with one instantaneous action, the samurai used to practise cutting arrows in flight, shot straight at them from a few tens of metres away. It is a form of training which is still used at the Maniwa-Nen ryu (a ball is attached to the ends of the arrows for protection). The great master, Higuchi Takizo, from the Maniwa-Nen ryu faces the bowman. (five times).

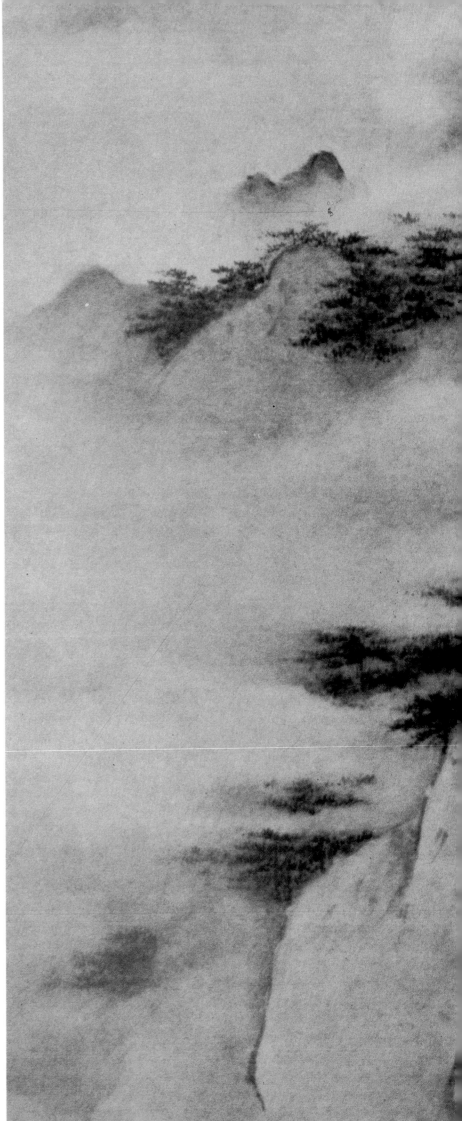

The art of the sword and the art of painting described by a Chinese master

The art of painting is also a search for unity and an expression of energy. Contemplation of nature can encourage the realization of the Void.

An old Chinese master, on meeting a young painter in the forest, asked:
— Do you know how to paint?
— You ignorant old peasant, what do you know about painting?
— How can you tell what is in my heart? said the master.
The young man felt surprised and ashamed.
— The first condition necessary for painting, said the master, is to follow the six basic rules and these same rules apply to the art of the sword.

The first is called 'qi' (spirit or vital energy); the second 'yun' (agreement or harmony); the third 'si' (thought or design); the fourth 'jing' (landscape effect); the fifth 'bi' (brush) and the sixth 'mo' (ink). The spirit enables thought to follow the movement of the brush and to determine the shape of things without hesitating. Harmony is the result of correct and perfect shapes. Thought brings out the essential element in these shapes. The landscape is formed by observing the law of the seasons. The brush must adhere to the rules while maintaining freedom and spontaneity of movement; in such a way that all things appear animated and mobile. The ink can be heavy or light, thick or thin, according to the depth and smoothness of things; the colour must be so natural that it hardly seems like the work of brushes.
An exemplary accomplished painter makes no effort to express variations in nature spontaneously. A profound painter's thoughts penetrate the nature of everything in heaven and earth. The skilful painter is characterized by the brush which obeys him (without thought). He says that reality is not enough for him, but he knows nothing about spontaneous movement, nor about 'qi'.

(From a story of the Sung period.)

Trees on peaks representing the Huashan mountains in northern China – by Wan Li (Ming era 1368-1644).

White sticks

Araki-Ryu is possibly the last remaining ryu where the art of the white sticks is practised.
Half way between the bokken and the shinai in kendo, white sticks are relatively dangerous. Yet, the only protection worn consists of long thick gloves and a sort of large padded headgear, shielding the skull and the ears.

157

Kendo

Origins of kendo

The teaching of kenjutsu (or art of the sword) was considered to be dangerous. It was not unusual during the course or even during practice kata, for the participants – masters and pupils alike – to be seriously wounded, maimed, or even killed.

So, it was necessary to adopt protective armour. The first designs were the work of several great masters of the Edo era (1603-1867), including Toranishi Kanshin and Ono Tadaaki.

The armour, inspired by that worn by great generals, included a helmet (kabuto) to protect the head and back of the neck, whilst the shoulders, chest, arms and hands were fitted with leather or metal guards.

Ono also invented an artificial sword made of bamboo strips. This was the forerunner of the shinai used in kendo today.

One of his pupils, Nakanishi Chuta, added to and improved Master Ono's efforts in about 1750. He invented the sword glove (or kote) and remodelled the artificial sword into a supple yet strong version made of four strips of bamboo and called a shinai.

Nakanishi Chuta himself founded a new tradition: the Itto-Ryu, in which all the pupils were compelled to wear armour and carry a shinai. The great advantage was that, as the pupil could be confident of striking without wounding, he could concentrate his efforts on the force and rapidity of his blows, so making considerable progress in a short time. Eventually, in spite of some reservations, all the other ryu in Japan in turn adopted the shinai.

Therefore, by 1760, young samurai pupils could choose between the wooden sword (or bokken), the shinai, or the deadly, traditional sword blade.

However, the first shinai made up of 32 pieces of reed covered in a heavy linen, distinctly lacked flexibility. Nakanishi simplified the first by joining together four strips

Master Takano's kendo pupils.

of bamboo. It seems that the perfect design had been found as this design is the same as the one used today. A tsuba or shield made of thick leather was fixed to the handle of the shinai.

The shinai's length and weight were strictly defined: 37.8–39in (96–9cm), and 3lb (1.36kg). The protective armour complete consists of: a helmet to protect the head and face (*men*); over the *hakama* and the *keikogi* (tunic and trousers worn in training) a new garment made of heavy stitched cotton is worn to protect the hips: the *tare;* over the tare, the *do* or breastplate is fitted.

This new protective armour necessitated a fresh method of approach. So, kenjutsu was named kendo (from do: the way, and ken: sword – in other words, the Way of the sword).

However, it was not until 1873 that kendo lost its guarded educational image.

The abolition of feudalism in 1870 had cast bushido arts into a sort of oblivion for a few years. Nevertheless, public kendo demonstrations organized by former samurai had roused a keen interest, all the more so because until then, all demonstrations, even straightforward training in sword practice and kendo, had been strictly prohibited to the public.

In view of its success, a law passed in 1871 made the teaching of kendo compulsory in all Japanese schools.

In 1909 the first college of the Kendo Federation was founded; in 1928, the general Federation was set up and ever since it has awarded grades as follows:

Shodan = first grade
Nidan = second grade
Sandan = third grade
Yodan = fourth grade
Godan = fifth grade
Rokudan = sixth grade
Shichidan = seventh grade
Hachidan = eighth grade
Kudan = ninth grade
Judan = tenth grade

Before becoming a 1st Dan or grade, the pupil must pass six kyu (or lower grades). It takes two to three years to become a 1st Dan. After the rank of 5th Dan, the coveted titles of *renshi,* then *kyoshi* and finally *hanshi* (or great master) are awarded according to personal merit.

Kendo training.

Kendo

In kendo, all the rules of sword fighting apply and are observed. It is said that the shinai is clothed in the spirit of the sword. Here, the great Master Tomihara is seen surrounded by his pupils.

The kendoka must not use his strength, in spite of the violence of the attack, punctuated with sensational kiai. In fact, what matters most is the technique of dealing the blow, control of the fingers and wrist and the combined movements of the legs and body. The stunning blow of the master kendoist stems from these factors. Here, pupils repeatedly practise blows or suburi. The concept of kendo is to discipline the human mind by means of applying the sword principles (katana).

The object of kendo practice is to train the body and mind, to build a strong soul, to strive relentlessly for improvement in the art of kendo by tough, serious training; to respect human courtesy and honour; to mix with others in all sincerity; and always strive for personal accomplishment.
(*Definition by the Japanese Kendo Federation.*)

Equipment

The size, length and weight of the shinai are given in the chart below (the weight of the tsuba is not included in that of the shinai).

Age	Size
13, 14, 15	37
16, 17, 18	38
19 and over	39

Length	Weight
44in (112cm)	13–16oz (375–450g)
45in (115cm)	16–17oz (450–485g)
46in (118cm)	over 17oz (485g)

If two shinai are used, the first should have a maximum length of 43in (110cm) and a minimum weight of 13oz (375g), whilst the second should have a maximum length of 24in (60cm) and a minimum weight of 9oz (265g). The tsuba is usually leather but can also be made of plastic. It is round with a maximum diameter of 3in (8cm). It must be securely fitted.

Putting on the protective clothing

The protective clothing consists of four items:
— Men (helmet)
— Kote (gloves)
— Do (breastplate)
— Tare (stomach guard)

These items of equipment are put on in the following order: first, the tare, which protects

the lower part of the abdomen and the hips, is fitted round the waist and tied in front like an apron; then the do, the breastplate, is fitted to the chest and held in place by strings passed over the shoulders and across the back; then the men, the helmet, is put over the head and tied at the back of the neck (underneath the men a stiff piece of material called a tenugi or hachimaki is placed on the hair); finally, the kote or gloves are put on, and, with the shinai, one is ready to begin.

Beginning, interruption and end of a contest

A fight begins by the referee declaring 'hajime' and is interrupted by the call 'yame'.

A fight ends when the referee declares 'shobu ari' (end of the contest) or 'hikiwake' (a draw) or 'shobu' (there is a winner).

The normal length of time allowed for a fight is three minutes. The time which elapses (a) between the referee declaring a point scored and the restarting of the contest, (b) when accidents occur or the referees need to consult each other, (c) between the orders to stop and restart the contest, is not counted as being part of the fight. However, the time the referee requires to separate two contestants in the tsuba zeriai position (in which they are very close together with their shinai and tsuba touching) is counted in the time allowed.

Points of attack

— Men: forehead.
Sho-men (middle forehead), migi-men (right of forehead), hidari-men (left of forehead).
— Kote: forearm.
Migi-kote (right forearm), hidari-kote (left forearm), in the following instances: chudan position where the left hand is in front; jodan position; hasso position; wakigamae position; the moment where the left hand comes in front of the right; and in other variations of the chudan position.
— Do: side.
Migi-do (right side); hidari-do (left side).
— Tsuki: throat (not permissible as a point of attack for contestants under 16 years of age).

Striking

Shinai sword fighting is governed by the law of kikentai no uchi, which can be described in terms of a successful blow using the body, the sword and the cry.

When striking, these three things must all come together at once. When one ingredient is missing or inadequate, the blow is not a good one and there can be no 'ippon'.

Assessing the blows

Good blows are delivered in well defined places using the upper third of the shinai. Blows to the throat (tsuki) are dealt with the point of the shinai; single-handed blows (katate) must be particularly precise. In all circumstances, the contestant must be fired with an intense spirit of attack and keep his body in a certain position. Points can also be awarded for the following blows:

1. A blow struck promptly to a contestant who has dropped his shinai or who has himself fallen over; similarly, a contestant who has just fallen can strike his opponent immediately after his own fall.
2. A blow dealt at the very moment the signal is given to end the fight.

Children's kendo.

From the age of three or four, boys and girls can learn kendo. The oldest of Master Takano's 80 young pupils is only seven.

The training takes place on the beach, far from the noises of the town. In this way, the children learn to discipline themselves at an early age.

Every session starts with a period of meditation lasting about ten minutes. Beforehand, the children greet the master and recite together:

'We love our country
We respect our parents
We respect the ceremony of our traditions
We respect our education
We will fulfil our duty
We respect our friends
We promise to cultivate healthy minds and bodies.'

1. Migi-do: blow to the right side of the breastplate

2/3. Hidari-do: blow to the left side

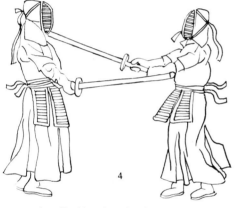

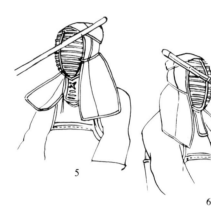

4. Tsuki: stab at the throat

5. Hidari-men: blow to the left side of the men
6. Migi-men: blow to the right side of the men
7. Men: blow to the middle of the head

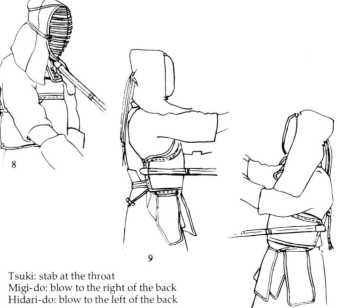

8. Tsuki: stab at the throat
9. Migi-do: blow to the right of the back
10. Hidari-do: blow to the left of the back

2. CORRECT METHOD OF HOLDING THE SHINAI

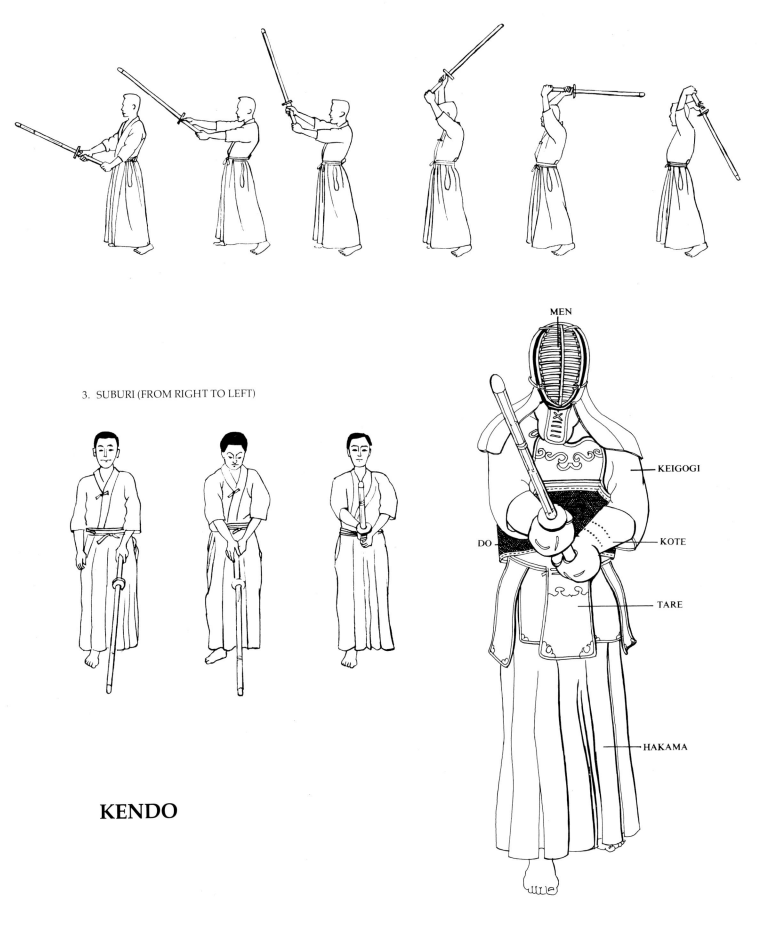

3. SUBURI (FROM RIGHT TO LEFT)

MEN

KEIGOGI

DO

KOTE

TARE

HAKAMA

KENDO

4. KENDO ARMOUR

165

Master Takano and sword kata. Here, Master Takano Kosei from Kamakura (9th Dan) opposes another master. This type of combat using the sword is restricted to those who have attained the highest rank in kendo.

Note in particular one of the fundamental rules of all martial arts: it concerns the eyes.
'In order to anticipate the opponent's actions, one must at the same time see, yet not see him', emphasizes Master Takano, 'he must be transparent; one must look at him as one views a mountain from a distance.'

From the rovings of the knight to the kendo of today

A sociable and traditional aspect of kendo is that as soon as they become *renshi*, adherents of the art often tour Japan, going from one dojo (training room) to the next. This custom, practised since the time of the samurai who, in the same way, travelled around the country passing through some of the most famous armouries, is called *mushashugyo*, meaning 'the rovings of the knight'.

Today, kendo is practised by over two million people in Japan. It has spread to the United States and to ten European countries. Outside the United States, kendo is established in Brazil, Argentina, the Philippines, Korea, Taiwan, Australia, etc. Holland, Belgium, Sweden, Germany, Yugoslavia, Switzerland, Italy and Austria also have kendo dojo, with England in the lead, having the first open dojos in Europe. The European Kendo Federation embodies the majority of national committees. An International Kendo Federation is made up of representatives from 20 countries including Japan.

From the sporting aspect, there have been three world kendo championships: 1970, Tokyo and Osaka, Japan; 1973, Los Angeles and San Francisco, USA; 1976, London, Great Britain.

The spirit of the samurai

Kendo reflects the spirit of the samurai whose aim was to approach and cut through their opponent at the first attempt. The technique therefore requires a combination of swiftness, strength and suppleness in order to strike this single theoretical blow which promptly decides the winner. At the moment of attack, a formidable cry, the kiai, is uttered. This cry from the stomach is harsh and terrifying. In kendo, the kiai requires a special training: the kiai-keiko. The force of the kiai tends to paralyse the opponent for a fraction of a second, just long enough for the shinai to strike home.

The four fundamental ways of striking an opponent with a sword are also used in kendo:
— *from top to bottom:* the sword splits open the opponent's head, possibly even his whole body
— *from left to right* (or vice versa to cut through the neck)
— *sideways* (to cut through the opponent at waist level).

The only thrust permissible allows the throat to be stabbed with the blade (tsuki).

In kendo training, it is customary to declare *men* if one intends to hit the head, *do* for either side of the breastplate, *kote* for the right glove,

tsuki for the throat. Only blows aimed at the front or sides count, provided the shinai does not touch the opponent's shinai. The ideal method is to remain at a distance from the opponent while drawing him towards you. This establishes tactics of attack–defence as any attack can be instantaneously converted to a defence and vice versa, the ultimate objective being to deal the decisive fatal blow.

The extreme concentration required, the mobilization within a short space of time of all physical and mental energy, the swiftness and power needed in striking, together form an art as thrilling as it is exhausting. Like a leaping flame or a flash of lightning, the kendoka must learn to transmit his energy to the tip of the shinai. It is said that the blows received at the end of the shinai in some instances equal the speed of a bullet from a revolver. The great masters can strike with such lightness that the shinai scarcely seems to brush the opponent, who is nevertheless knocked down and defeated.

The supreme art involves remaining perfectly composed with total peace of mind, until springing into action at the very moment when the opponent is himself preparing to strike.

Fear must be overcome. As in kendo the object is to attack, receding or parrying are signs of weakness. The contestant is stretched to the limit of his capabilities. The fight is fast and ruthless. It is only when mentally and physically exhausted that one learns to deliver the blows in the correct way. Another force replaces the brute physical and mental force. This state called *kirikaeshi* gives, according to a Japanese proverb, 'ten virtues to the attacker and eight virtues to the recipient'.

Extreme concentration and the 'subtle' states

The great masters are able to make use of the moment of vulnerability. That is why it is said that the opponent must remain transparent, that one must at the same time see and yet not see the enemy, or look at him as one views a mountain from a distance.

According to a spiritual metaphor, the opponent is in the end the mirror of oneself. Therefore, kendo in its finality is an invitation to fight against oneself.

No doubt that is why meditation and silence play an important role in kendo: in order to attain the calmness of a millpond, it is necessary to achieve a state of mind free of thought and tension, an entirely peaceful inner being and total detachment. Moreover, the state of mind in which one must not allow oneself to be interrupted by any movement or incident whatsoever, is called 'clear mirror, quiet water' in Japanese.

Similarly, the expression 'the reflection of the moon in the water' implies the state of him who, being a true master, has acquired an internal harmony like a subtle marriage between the moon's reflection and the water.

In kendo, more so than in any other discipline, the rule of complementary effects is noticeable: the extreme tension in kendo can only be attained by doing the opposite. So kendo, heir to the great way of the sword, has an ultimate significance in the union of opposites: life and death, the being and the non-being. Even the cry used in kendo, the kiai, is recognized as a unifying force combining mind, body and sword. It can be said that the entire physical body – legs, hips and arms – is totally committed in kendo and likewise all the spiritual functions.

The very fact of acting on time and space gives kendo a characteristic notion of time-space united in a single concept known as *ma-ai*.

Finally, the shinai represents the single vector of these forces, unifying them and concentrating them on one spot. This very spot is the ultimate goal which determines the way of a progression, at the end of which the shinai and the fight are mere instruments of a different and inexpressible awareness of life itself.

Kendo training.

Attack: shinai against shinai.

Master Takano meditating in his dojo.

Suburi: raising and lowering the shinai.

Master Takano surrounded by his pupils.

Naginata

Madame Shimada

To discover the great tradition of the naginata-do, one must go to the Jikishin-kage Ryu run by Madame Shimada where the tradition in its purest form is displayed.

Although as a sport, naginata-do is practised almost exclusively by women, many ryu including Maniwa-Nen, Katori or Araki-Ryu, still practise naginata-jutsu according to the old rules.

The naginata or halberd

The naginata is a weapon made from 2 to 3 yards of hard wood, at the end of which is a blade about 12in (30cm) long and as sharp as a sword. In some cases, the blade could be from 24in (60cm) to over 1 yard long. The naginata is derived from the 'kwanto' or Chinese bronze halberds imported very early on.

In the Nara period, it was difficult to combat armed warriors – an increasingly important fighting force – with classical weapons such as arrows or swords. The length of the naginata, however, enabled foot soldiers to hamstring the horses and keep the knights at bay.

In the famous battle of the Taira versus the Minamoto at Dan-No-Ura (1185), the naginata played an important role. From that time on, its use on battle fields became widespread and many samurai lost their legs.

Naginata ryu in Japan increased in number. In the Muromachi era (1336-1574) there were 425 but during this time fire arms were introduced (1542) and gradually relegated the naginata, as well as the sword, to a position of secondary importance.

Since the Heian era, the naginata has been used in teaching samurai women and monk-warriors. (The skill and prowess of some women fighters have gone down in history.) Since the time of the Tokugawa, the use of the naginata has been left exclusively to women. Today, the Naginata Federation comprises about 400,000 to 500,000 devotees throughout the world.

Naginata

In Japan, naginata-do has been almost exclusively adopted by women. They have made it into a popular and widely practised sport.

174

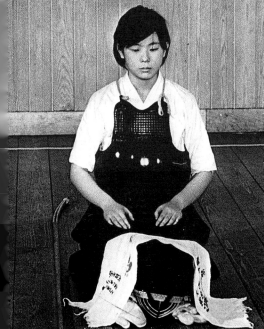

These young girls being trained in the use of the naginata at the budokan dojo in Tokyo have to wear a protective armour when fighting, similar to that worn in kendo.

Combat between naginata and kenjutsu. Maniwa-Nen ryu.

Naginata, in its turn, has become a *do* (art) and, as such is taught in schools. In some old country ryu, such as Araki-Ryu, men, women and children actively pursue naginata-jutsu.

Allied to kendo (having copied the protective armour), naginata comprises about 25 combat techniques. Its long and difficult training takes four to five years.

In battle, naginata involved circular sweeping movements calculated by centrifugal force. The weapon made a clean sweep, cutting down everything around it with remarkable force.

Tournaments in which kendo and naginata compete frequently take place and it must be said that the naginata often has the advantage.

Three ryu practise naginata-do, the most important being the Jikishin-kage Ryu, followed by the Toda-Ha-Buko Ryu and the Tendo Ryu.

Drawing by Siebold depicting samurai weapons (1 and 2: musket, 3, 4, 5 and 6: kendo, 7: yari).

176

Yari

The yari or spear

Of the other different types of spear, we shall describe the yari which has a shorter shaft than the naginata and a blade about 8in (20cm) long, with two cutting edges, allowing two-way attack (cutting tendons, knees, etc.)

Also called a yari is a spear about 4yds long and seldom used because of its awkward handling. Another type of spear was made of a long pole with a cruciform at the end made of two cutting blades fixed perpendicular to the handle. The point of the weapon used in training is made of wood protected by a leather ball and two round wooden bars take the place of the blades.

This ancient weapon was used to knock down the enemy by cutting smartly through his legs. By swinging the blades back and forth, one could also cut through the neck, arms, sides, leg joints, knees, etc.

Yari, or 4yd spear.
Maniwa-Nen ryu.

An engraving which illustrates training in a ryu. Despite Western influence, this engraving gives a fairly accurate idea of the atmosphere in a true traditional ryu, as can be seen if one compares it with the photo on the left taken at the Maniwa-Nen ryu.

The bokken or wooden sword

The effectiveness of the wooden sword or bokken is demonstrated by Musashi's famous fight against his father's murderer, Sasaki. Musashi knew that Sasaki used a very long straight sword, so he cut himself a wooden sword from a pole, slightly longer than Sasaki's.

During the fight, as Musashi had predicted, Sasaki's sword reached as far as Musashi's forehead but only cut through the cotton band protecting his head. His bokken on the other hand reached as far as Sasaki's head, killing him.

Since the Ashikaga era, the bokken has increasingly taken the sword's place in competitions, thus reducing the number of injuries and deaths. It is actually modelled on a real sword (whilst the bo and jo are rounded staves). Nowadays, it has become a training aid in many budo disciplines, including karate and aiki-do.

Sword duel. Drawing by Hokusai.

Demonstration of bokken fighting between old masters. Note the protective glove, rarely used.

Bokken

Children from the Maniwa-Nen ryu advancing, armed with bokken.

Bo

The bo or staff

The primitive use of long staves or short sticks (*bo* and *jo*) is appreciably diminishing as time goes by. Yet, in Japan, the staff has shown considerable growth in popularity (bojutsu schools have numbered as many as 316).

There is therefore a great variety of teaching methods involving an equally wide range of staves. For the record, we shall quote the *kyushakubo,* about 3yds (2.80m) long, from Okinawa and the *rokushakubo,* 2yds (1.80m) long, made of very hard oak. The Katori ryu has developed the staff into an effective weapon for use against all types of swords. The training comprises a dozen techniques taught in strict sequence, requiring several years of practice.

The bo's effectiveness in the hands of an expert is exceptional. By sliding it through the hand, the length of the staff can vary instantaneously; in addition, far from striking with the tip alone, the bo describes complex and often uncheckable figures.

Bo training takes place in the open air without any special form of protection. During the first few months, the pupil must assimilate the figures (or kata) and the different positions. Two-man combat is only introduced very much later.

The art of the staves
Bo or staff

Ancient warriors considered the techniques of the short stick (jo) and the long staff (bo) to be of secondary importance but they still learnt the method and the practice. The Katori ryu raised the staff to the dignity of a true fighting weapon. The monk-warriors of the 16th century made it their chosen weapon because they said that the staff's humility could make it powerful and so conquer the enemy, or even break the famous sword in two.

This formidable samurai armed with an enormous studded staff is Benkei the giant, the celebrated hero who, with his master Yoshitsune of the Minamoto clan, crushed the Taira in the 13th century.

183

Jo

The jo or short stick

The history of the short stick or *jo* is allied to one of the most moving stories concerning the martial arts.

There was once a samurai called Muso Gonnosuke. He was a very famous samurai who knew how to use a vast number of weapons but who was particularly attached to the staff. He had studied the *bo* technique in depth, first at the Katori ryu and then at the Kashima.

Armed with the bo, he roamed Japan, challenging the greatest masters and never suffering defeat, and so came to Edo (Tokyo today). His fame spread until the day Miyamoto Musashi took up the gauntlet.

Muso attacked, but with an even swifter and more sudden movement Musashi parried the blow with his sword and threatened his opponent's life. However, Musashi did

Masters of Aikido practising Jo

not want to take advantage of his victory, and let Muso go.

This defeat threw Muso into the depths of despair. For years he tried in vain to think of a way to remedy it and overcome Musashi.

Eventually, he went to Kyushu in the south of Japan and took refuge at the top of a mountain where, for several months, he forced himself to lead a life of meditation and asceticism.

His enlightenment occurred during one sleepless night. He immediately began to make a new much shorter stick out of a very hard wood, which he called the *jo*. He thought that this short stick would enable him to get closer to his opponent and to concentrate his blows on the vulnerable points of the body (atemi).

Muso perfected a series of twelve basic movements and named his new skill *jojutsu*. And so, the technique of the short stick was born.

Muso still wanted his revenge against Musashi and a new encounter took place. This time, the impossible happened: Musashi, who had until then remained unconquered, suffered the only defeat of his life and Muso emerged the winner. But, as Musashi had spared him, Muso gave him his life.

Once jojutsu had been accepted into the family of martial arts, it continued to assert itself – particularly during the Tokugawa period when there was an increasing tendency to confront adversaries without killing them.

Nevertheless, the practice remained secret until the Meiji era and it was only in 1955 that it lost its fighting image and became in its turn a *do* under the name of jodo.

Yet, many ryu allied to the Shindo-Muso-Ryu zealously preserve the techniques of jojutsu, whilst a Federation has formed around jodo, attached to the Kendo Federation.

The practice of jo, although seemingly easy, requires many years of training. As in bo, no protection is worn. A characteristic of these two weapons is that they are, more often than not, used in the open air and they require great dexterity, or a certain amount of courage, if one is not to fear the blows.

The most comprehensive teaching of jojutsu, practised at the Shindo-Muso-Ryu, comprises 64 techniques. They are all taught in progressive order. At least ten years' practice is required to become a great master of jo.

The jo or short stick. The Katori ryu singles out 12 techniques for the short stick, of which six are taught initially. The other six are brought in at a higher level. No protection is worn in training, so much skill and courage is required and figure practice essential. Here, Master Otake from the Katori ryu trains with Donn Draeger.

The Way of breathing and of

empty hands

Throw by Master Yamaguchi.

The flowing suppleness of aiki-do, keeping a stable body centre, the art of using the opponent's energy, that of never being off balance, all these rules can only be obeyed by virtue of a profound unity: this unity is called music or breath. And the master says that the breath is none other than that of the universe. Here, the master will repel five opponents at once.

Aiki-do is above all the art of controlling the body and all forms of life, with the mind.

Master Yamaguchi carries to perfection the art of obeying the laws of the circle.

Naked couple walking towards the setting sun, a symbol of yin and yang (*previous pages*).

The art of breathing or respiration, primarily a Chinese Way

However far back you go in Indian and Chinese history, you find the idea by which man, through the science of breathing, enters into harmony with the five elements, man himself being an image of these five elements.

The theory of the five elements is infinitely complex in its relationships of complement and agreement: the five planets act on the five elements, which in turn act on the five colours, the five parts of the body, the five vowels and the five sounds.

This type of understanding can become a game for scholars or, on the other hand, a profound initiation which reveals in 'Tao' (or Dao) the vital principle of the elements of the universe, that which is the breath of life, the energy emanating from and penetrating all things. Man can do nothing so long as he does not appreciate the visible and invisible effects of this energy or this breath which embraces both himself and the universe. Everything is united in the Chinese thought: the moral order and the natural order, the natural and the supernatural.

The sense of dao, meaning 'way' or 'path' (which can be likened to the Japanese *do* meaning the same thing, or the Way in budo) can be found as early as two or three centuries BC in China. In actual fact, dao expresses the movement of two complementary forces, yin and yang, the combined action of which drives the universe in all its most varied forms: life and death, summer and winter, day and night, etc. This duality is nothing but a continuous movement with interdependent aspects.

If body and mind are one, the development of physical and mental capabilities can in a way be unlimited, provided they are united and controlled. With this in mind, in about 600 a Buddhist monk called Bohidharma started a new trend in the Shaolin temple in China from which probably stemmed most of the rules and concepts which largely govern all martial arts.

The legendary Chinese emperor Fou Hi (2000 BC) is said to have invented the cooking of food and the eight trigrammes (*pa-kua*) which enable all the elements of the cosmos to be classified and related to the primordial forces of nature. He represents a pre-agricultural period of Chinese civilization of which he is considered to be the founder.

The sequence of the two principles (yin-yang), depicted as straight even lines or broken uneven ones, made it possible to build up eight trigrammes (*pa-kua*) using sticks, some of which had a concave (yang) and others a convex edge (yin).

Bodhisattva and the Dragon–Tang period (618-907) by Lu Lengjia. The dragon is symbolic of the untamed vital forces.

Between 1260 and 1368 BC there lived in China a wise man called Sahng (or Sanfeng), to whom the creation of T'ai-Chi (or Taiji) is attributed.

T'ai-Chi is a method of controlling actions and breathing. The exercises, as we know them today, can combine extreme slowness and extreme quickness. A devotee of T'ai-Chi by definition understands the Void, to the point where he becomes fluid and intangible like the air itself.

This fluidity must be such that 'the addition of a feather changes your weight', said an old master, or that a 'bird placed in your hand can not find the small amount of support needed underfoot in order to fly off'.

This sums up the distant and probable origin of what one can call the *Way of breathing and of empty hands,* which incorporates aiki-do, karate, judo and sumo. In spirit, there is no fight, or rather only Breath exists and the hands when in action are an extension of the Breath. In actual fact, no discipline can be excluded from this principle. However, aiki-do, karate and judo have made it into a fundamental rule.

Birds on branches in
autumn, by Jen Jen Fa
(1254-1327). Yuan
period.

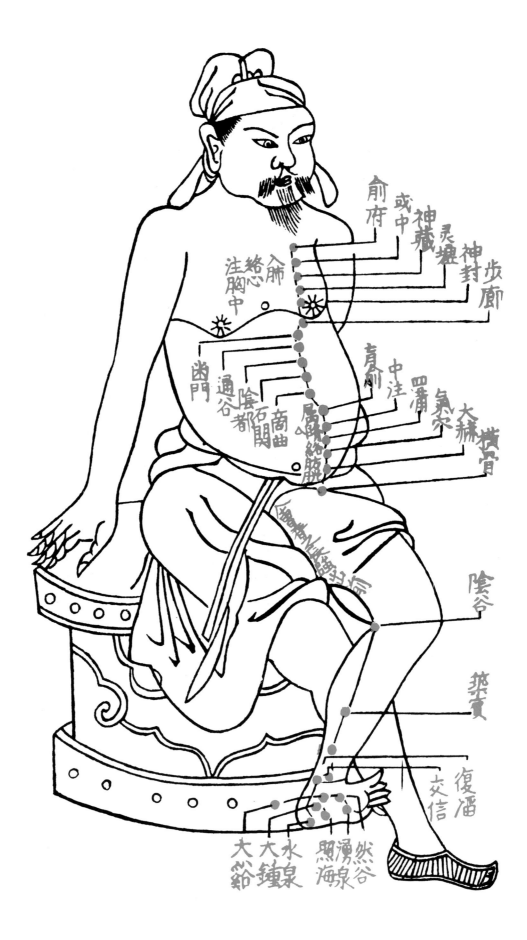

俞府 或中 神藏 灵墟 神封 步廊

注胸 俞肺 幽門 通谷 陰都 石關 商曲 盲俞 絡肬 肓俞 中注 四滿 氣穴 大赫 橫骨

陰谷

筑賓

復溜 交信

大谿 大鍾 水泉 照海 湧泉 然谷

The circuits

The energy circuits or meridians in Chinese acupuncture are no longer disputed by modern science. These once mysterious circuits revealed by up-to-date measuring equipment, prove that the age-old conception of ki and its yin and yang polarity is true.

Ibuki

Master Shiokawa teaches a form of respiration called ibuki which stops one feeling pain. The respiration comes from the stomach. Mastery of this respiration enables one to control body and mind come what may. It is therefore a fundamental application.

Again, it can be said that there is control of respiration at the beginning and that there is control of respiration at the end; between the two, the sudden rapid attack has expressed the Breath.

Understanding the Breath means: transforming respiration into concentration, concentration into energy, energy being a dimension of time: the opponent, stretched to his limits, is struck or thrown because your time is infinitely quicker than his.

Respiration is extended into action in the sense that energy penetrates and intersects the action. There is Breath precisely because energy cannot stop at an obstacle. In spirit, a spurt of energy sweeps aside the obstacle and continues. For a master, the opponent does not exist; he is merely an obstacle on the course.

This method of expression involves a finality which is the privilege of a few masters. Nevertheless, if at the outset one does not envisage the possible and virtually unlimited horizon of a voyage, what is the good of undertaking the trip?

Everything happens as though control of respiration enabled one to discover deeper and more subtle ways of breathing, inexpressible ways of relating art to energy, in other words not breathing in the ordinary sense through the chest but practising respiration of the mind (which is awareness and serenity), respiration of the limbs and one could go so far as to speak of respiration of the blood itself, in the sense that mastery of breathing leads to perfectly balanced mastery over the heart and circulation of the blood.

Master Shiokawa Terushige directs more than 3000 pupils from Shimonoseki (southern Japan). He is an all-round master. Although he prefers karate, like the ancient samurai he knows all the martial arts, He is also an accomplished master of the sai, sword and staves.

The 'point of gravity' in judo, aiki-do and karate

Karate is determined by one's will to concentrate the greatest amount of energy in one spot; judo too acts on a single point but by shifting the centre of gravity. As soon as the vertical line which passes through the centre of gravity is moved outside the area of support, the subject is ready to fall. In aiki-do, the point is the centre of a circle. Any change of position pulls the opponent towards the void symbolized by this centre and makes him fall.

The open or empty hands

The expression 'empty hands' is peculiar to the karate of Okinawa, the word karate itself meaning 'empty hands'. A second meaning is added to the literal sense. The empty hand is also the hand free of nervous tension and restriction, the hand through which the energy passes. In aiki-do, the position of the open hand, with outstretched fingers is called tegatana. Here, the hand is the image of energy itself which can indifferently determine life or death, and be yin or yang, the negative or positive force.

Similarly in judo, the hand is the extension of the intelligence combined with technique. Master Kano's judo had to be like a dance. That meant that only he who possessed suppleness of mind and body could attack properly. The hand penetrated the opposing force and in a way attracted this force to it in order to use it and throw it.

Karate still obeys the same principle adapted to the total mobilization of energy transmitted by the hand.

Fear and the spirit of sacrifice

If the spirit of power and the search for strength come last in all the skills using 'empty hands', then the spirit of sacrifice which consists of overcoming fear, comes

One of Master
Shikowa's pupils
practising karate kata.

first. It is obvious that all fear paralyses, restrains and hinders the flow of movement, whatever it might be. The object of every martial art is never effectiveness, for there can be no effectiveness if fear is present. The object is therefore to overcome fear. The following was sung by a master of the Kamakura period:[1]

[1] Quoted by J. L. Jazarin in *The Spirit of Judo,* published (in French) by Le Pavillon.

'The bow is broken, the arrows are gone
At this critical moment
A feeble heart does not like to beat
with power and force
When a pointed arrow is released
From a loosely strung bow, it will surely pierce the king.'

Another master said: 'He who hangs on is certain to fall, but he who does not hang on need have no fear of falling.'

Kangeiko or winter training.

Most karate masters undergo winter training or kangeiko. For eight days during the coldest part of the year, wearing only light linen suits, they meditate at the water's edge before entering the sea and holding proper contests.

Kata.

There are about 60 kata or figures in karate (of which about 40 at most can be practised). Here in the grounds of a Shinto temple at Shimonoseki, karate pupils carry out an impressive series of these figures, all perfectly synchronized and very beautiful to watch. The five basic kata are sufficient to face any situation. The origin of the kata is Chinese. Funakoshi Gichin imported them from Okinawa. He knew how to adapt and simplify a large number of these figures. The essential elements of karate are expressed in the kata.

Karate training and kata

Master Shiokawa watching a karate training session.

In judo, fearless attack with 'self-sacrifice' is called *sutemi*. In slightly differing forms, the same concept is true of aiki-do and karate.

The aspects common to all three Ways are countless, for the basis of application consists of the same principles in different forms. Of course, the closer one gets to these forms, the more apparent the differences, and the more one relates to the fundamental spirit, the less perceptible they become.

The way of empty hands could be called 'way of controlling energy', in the sense of subtle energy which has mastered primary energy of a muscular and physiological nature which every well-built man possesses.

In each of these disicplines, the techniques are there like as many steps in a staircase open to the horizon where movement, force and spirit are synonymous with the freedom of being.

Aiki-do

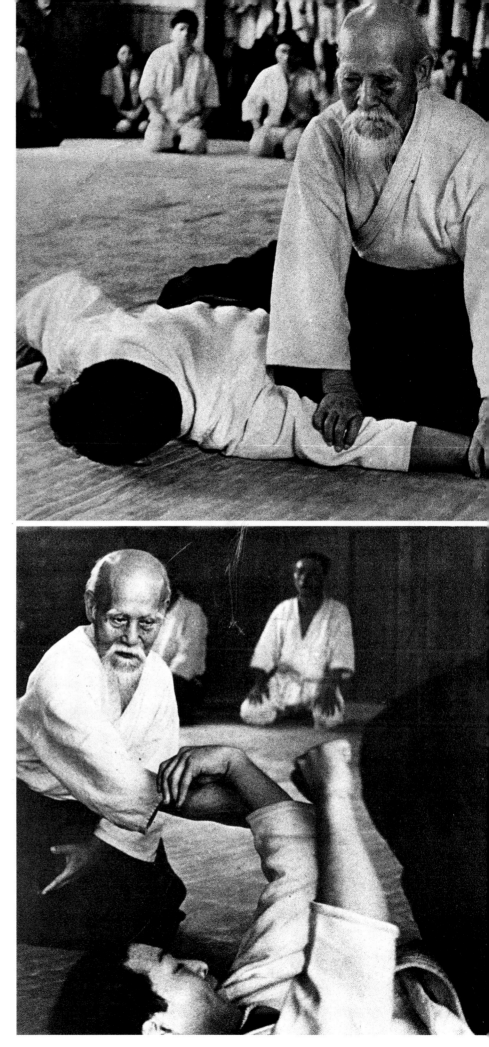

The life of Master Ueshiba Morihei: acquiring strength

On 14 December 1883, Ueshiba Morihei was born in Tanabe, a small town near Osaka. His father was a master of swordsmanship in the Kii family, lords of the province.

Until the age of 15, Ueshiba Morihei had a weak constitution. His small size and lack of physical resistance meant he could get little benefit from his father's teaching.

When he was 13, he met his first master, Tozawa Tokusaburo from the Kito ryu, who taught him jujutsu. So he very soon learnt to wield the spear and the sword. At 20, he was already recognized as an expert in these skills (1908) and received a diploma from his master Nakai Masakatsu, when he left the great ryu, Yagyu.

Ueshiba Morihei swore to himself that he would become strong and that he would spare no effort in achieving this aim. At the age of 20, he could already lift enormous weights and feared only a few opponents.

When the Russo-Japanese war broke out in Manchuria, Ueshiba was 21. He volunteered for service and was enrolled as a regular soldier. These years gave him the opportunity to strengthen his body with the toughest of tests. He withstood it so well that his exceptional conduct and his strength, which seemed indomitable, opened wide the doors to a military career.

But once the war was over, Ueshiba's aim was to resume his interrupted studies in jujutsu, as quickly as possible. However, his health broke down and he was confined to bed for six months, suffering from a serious attack of encephalitis. On his recovery, he took up judo.

The need for a change of air, to rediscover nature, cultivate the land and above all to strengthen his body, persuaded him to move to the north of Japan, to the island of Hokkaido. He was then 27. A year later, a meeting took place which was to alter the course of his life.

Master Ueshiba Morihei teaching in his dojo at Iwama.

201

Master Ueshiba with Katana

'Nobody can take away my strength since I do not use it,' used to say Master Ueshiba. 'The best technique is to avoid combat.'

Demonstration by the master showing the power of the hara.

When one of his pupils tries to push him using all the strength of his body and head, the master remains impassive, smiling and showing no sign of any effort of resistance. Neither would the combined strength of several men have any effect. The master's shoulders and arms are completely relaxed. If someone pushed him from behind, he would continue to concentrate his mind on the point (hara). He has no thought for the pushing action nor for the one doing the pushing. Concentration on the hara creates a stable and serene strength.

The origin of aiki-do and the cost of learning

This was a meeting with Master Sokaku from the Daito jujutsu ryu.

Master Takeda was a man of small build, of great strength and immensely tough and severe. He flattered himself with belonging to an ancient ancestral line, a branch of the famous Minamoto family. As for his teaching, he traced this back, according to a distant tradition, to Prince Sadazumi 874-916 (sixth son of Emperor Seiwa), who is said to have

been the founder of the first forms of aiki-jutsu at the Daito ryu. This secret teaching is said to have been passed on to Minamoto Yoshimitsu. As he lived in Takeda in the province of Kai, he took the name Takeda and henceforth, from generation to generation, the secret principles of aiki-jutsu have been passed on in the name of this family.

During the Meiji period, the head of the family, Takeda Sokaku, opened a private ryu in 1868, the Daito ryu, in distant Hokkaido. For the very first time, pupils outside the family could be accepted by the master. However, only distinguished people

Master Morihei
Ueshiba demonstrating
the short stick (here a
boar spear).

(members of the imperial family and some exceptional cases) were permitted the benefits of such instruction.

Takeda Sokaku was therefore above all a master conscious of both his importance and the value of what he had to impart. In Ueshiba Morihei, then aged 28, he recognized a person of exceptional skill and impressive self-control. He complimented him and accepted him as his pupil.

For all that, he did not give him an easy life. Ueshiba had to submit wholeheartedly to the extreme authoritarianism of the master to whom he had to devote body and soul, if necessary waiting on him at all hours of the day and night, preparing his meals, his baths, and even building him a new house. In addition, he had to pay the master between 300 and 500 yens for the teaching of each new technique, which was a large sum in those days.

Even so, the days spent in instruction were themselves infrequent. In five years, the master only devoted about a hundred days to it. The rest of the time, the pupil had to practise alone. Eventually, in 1916, at the age of 33, Ueshiba received the first diploma appointing him master of jujutsu at the Daito ryu.

The basic elements of modern aiki-do still stem from this teaching.

Meeting with Reverend Deguchi and death of his father

However, events gained momentum. First of all, Ueshiba Morihei, on learning that his father was dangerously ill, made a gift of all his property to his master, Takeda. Leaving behind the land he had made fertile, a village he had built and many warm friendships, he left Hokkaido for good. He was then 35.

On his return journey, Master Ueshiba heard about a man whose powers and great sense of spirituality were praised: the Reverend Deguchi Wanisaburo. He decided to change his route in order to go and visit him. Reverend Deguchi was the founder of a Shinto sect called *Omoto-Kyo*.

This meeting greatly influenced the life of Master Ueshiba. The centre of Omoto-Kyo was in Ayabe, in the district of Kyoto. When he arrived at his father's bedside, it was too late: his father was dead.

All these events deeply affected Morihei. He went to his father's tomb to pay his last respects. In a moment of intense emotion, he invoked the paternal spirit and swore that henceforth he would devote all his human and spiritual force to probing the secret of being and of budo.

A profound change took place in him. For four years, until he was about 41, he lived in solitary confinement. Faithful to tradition, Ueshiba selected a remote house in the holy mountain, at Ayabe. In Ayabe itself, he frequently met Reverend Deguchi with whom he shared great communion of spirit. For example, it is interesting to quote three of the rules laid down by Omoto-Kyo to enable its followers to get closer to God:

The master meditating in his garden at the age of 76. He possessed the harmony of all things because he had intelligence of soul. And every morning he would say, 'This soul is once again as good as new and again one starts offering it to one's brothers in life.'

1. Observe the true phenomena of nature and you will. be thinking of the *body* (substance) of the only true God.
2. Observe the impeccable working of the universe and you will be thinking of the *energy* of the only true God.
3. Observe the mentality of living beings and you will understand the *soul* of the only true God.

Reference to energy as a sign of God and creation signifies that the prime purpose of the universe is *vitality* and that all that exists is simply a demonstration of this vitality.

The understanding of this original and universal energy plays an essential and primordial part in aiki-do, in the form of *ki*.

205

Ki

According to the oriental concept, creation is merely the emanation of an original force or an omni-powerful energy, which, out of the chaos, progressively forms masses of dust particles or gas into planets, sun, moon, stars and galaxies. The evolution of this energy created the animal, mineral and vegetable world. If this primordial energy is called *ki,* all things stem from ki (*qi* in Chinese).

Being timeless, ki has no beginning and no end, it has no form but can assume any form. It is.

Aiki-do is defined by the way which relates man to the cosmic power, or ki. This idea of man, in harmony with the creative and original force of all things, is also at the root of life and serenity. 'He who discovers the secret of aiki-do', said Master Ueshiba, 'has the universe within him and can say "I am the universe".'

That which *is*, is absolute, lasting and timeless. Moreover, the master said 'That is why, when an enemy tries to fight me, he faces the universe itself, he must break its harmony. But the very moment he thinks he has got the measure of me, he is already beaten . . .' Because thought, be it slow or fast, is outside the limits of time.

A philosophy and a spirituality which, through aiki-do, have attained such a high degree of application, deserve to be followed. The master himself had been seduced by the profoundly humanitarian cosmic ideas of the Reverend Deguchi.

A trip to Mongolia

Deguchi nurtured the idea of unifying the moral and religious meaning of the world. In February 1934, he revealed a highly secret plan to Master Ueshiba and a handful of friends: to go to Mongolia where the Chinese and Japanese armies were engaged in conflict, in order to set up a Kingdom of Peace, by means of a Sino-Japanese alliance, so that the realization of the Kingdom of God could commence in Asia.

However fantastic and illusory such an ambition may have seemed, Reverend Deguchi had many advantages.

In actual fact, 'with the support of Tchang

Tso-Lin (or Zang Zuolin), then master of Mukden, he raised an "Independent Army of the North-West" which soon numbered ten or so units, and which he put under the command of General Lu Chan-kin (or Shangui). The sun, moon, stars and earth were all depicted on his "divine standard". Pillage was forbidden. Reverend Deguchi with his army roamed the Mongol plains heralding the Kingdom of God, healing the sick and handing out salt and rice. Unfortunately, his success disturbed Tchang Tso-Lin who withdrew his support, sent an army against him and had Lu-Chan-kin (or Lu Shangui) shot, together with the other Chinese officers.'[1] Master Ueshiba was himself captured. As he showed unusual strength of character and willpower, his enemies subjected him to all kinds of endurance tests, chained him up and tortured him. A forceful intervention on the part of the Japanese saved the whole troop just in time. Their return to Japan was greeted as a national event. As for Ueshiba Morihei, he returned to his remote house at Ayabe.

The awakening of a Sixth Sense and the heart of the universe

It was during this journey that the famous incident occurred, when Ueshiba was suddenly threatened with death by an enemy six yards away pointing a revolver at him. The man was promptly assaulted by Ueshiba and disarmed. When asked later how he had accomplished such a feat, Ueshiba is said to have replied: a very long time elapses between the moment a man decides to pull the trigger and the moment he actually does so. This event indicates that from that time on he had the ability to anticipate an enemy's thought and actions.

This sixth sense which only a few great masters actually manage to acquire, almost always goes with a deep inner experience which is difficult to describe. It seems that for a time, maybe a fraction of a second, the veil which divides the world of normal perception from that of profound reality suddenly ceases to exist. And this indescribable reality brings about a definitive change in the being. The following testimony by the master himself is just one of many accounts of similar experiences which enable one to sense a second imaginary level of reality beneath the surface.

[1] Quotation from Jean Herbert in *Japan's Popular Gods and Sects,* published (in French) by Albin Michel, p. 171.

The master meditating
prior to a bokken
demonstration.

In his dojo at Iwama, the master would rediscover communion with nature, just as before at Ayabe. This communion was prayer.

This event took place one day in Spring 1925 (when he was 42), whilst the master was walking in his garden . . .

Near a persimmon tree, it suddenly became impossible for him either to go forward or sit down. An intense heat came over him, causing his face to perspire heavily.

The master said, 'I had the sensation that the universe was suddenly shaking and that a gold-coloured spiritual energy, rising from the ground, shrouded my body in a veil, turning it gold. At the same time, my body and spirit became luminous. I could understand the chattering of birds and I had a clear comprehension of the intentions of God, the creator of the universe. At that moment, I was enlightened. I understood that the source of budo is the love of God, the spirit of loving protection of all creatures. Endless tears of joy ran down my cheeks.

'Since then, I have realized that the whole earth is my home, that the sun, moon and stars are all mine. I was freed of all desire, not only for my position, fame or prosperity but also for strength. I understood that budo does not consist of bringing down the enemy by force, nor is it a means to destroy the world with weapons: the pure spirit of budo means accepting the spirit of the universe, spreading peace throughout the world, speaking correctly, protecting and honouring all nature's creatures. I understood that the purpose of budo is to accept the love of God in its true sense which protects and cultivates all living things and that it is advisable to use and assimilate it with our mind and body.'

The master also said that 'the Way of budo is to make the heart of the universe one's own heart'.

During the summer of 1927, the master left the mountain at Ayabe with his family and went to live in Tokyo. His considerable fame preceded him and many great names and important well-known people hurried to his home to gain the favour of his teaching. The master formed a group of 30 to 40 pupils of whom most were already masters of judo and kendo.

aiki-do is the art of non-combat. However, as he was nevertheless attacked, Shirata threw his opponent, subdued him with one hand and said to him with good humour 'You see, can you resist a world of non-resistance?'

Many similar anecdotes illustrate the disbelief of powerful people, wrestling champions, sumotori, boxers, etc., to whom it was inconceivable that a man as small and delicate as the master could not be quickly crushed before their eyes. Inevitably, the opposite always happened: even before the blow they attempted reached its target, they were all without fail thrown by an uncontrollable force.

Today, in this very same dojo, his son, Master Kisshomaru Ueshiba, in turn comes to honour his father's memory before a small Shinto altar.

The master's dojo, called kobukan, became the centre of an exceptional training course. The intensity of the work which continued sometimes throughout the day and night, formed men of remarkable strength and character.

One of them, Shirata Rinjiro, was once challenged by two strong armed men to measure his powers in single combat. Shirata refused, pointing out that the very essence of

The secret of this power, bearing the master's words in mind, seemed inconceivable to the spirit. And yet, this force which is used precisely without force is none other than the energy of the universe. 'The movements in aiki-do', said the master, 'are the movements of nature, whose secret is profound and infinite.' To discover even a fragment of this secret is to understand inwardly that the man is himself the

209

From the symbol to cosmic energy.

The master liked to repeat the words: *maru, sankaku, shikaku,* meaning circles, triangles and squares; three words expressing an image and producing an energy.

The circle is none other than the cosmic universe, the square is the earth and the triangle, man. Through respiration or rather by ki, the circle, the square and the triangle, or sky, man and earth, are united.

The sounds

The esoteric understanding of aiki-do is extremely profound. Master Ueshiba devoted his life to it. One of the essential aspects of his research concerned the symbolic and the power of sounds. The five sounds of the creating are I, followed by E, A, O, U – I being the original sound corresponding to the Word of the Evangelist according to St John: 'In the beginning was the Word, the Word was God'. E A O U represent the four stages of the creation. These four stages are symbolic of the respiration rhythm of the universe. These four rhythms generate eight forces which are also the eight colours and the eight sounds. The figure eight in Japan and the East is the figure of infinity (8, 64, 512, 4096, up to infinity).
The four stages, U O A E, develop the original energy, and create the subjective and formal world. Each letter represents an aspect of being, the sounds represent the tangible universe. Beyond, only the rhythms exist (in other words, the intangible universe, the non-being, devoid of colours and sounds).
Each stage has its own vibrations, joining the spiritual essence to the physical body. By studying, not the causality but the relationship between the stages, one can comprehend the Way (michi), that is to say, that which units I – the intangible – to WI – the tangible.
The four stages of the creation, multiplied by the eight forces, generate the 32 states of reality.
This very summary explanation, which is therefore open to criticism, is only given as an indication to make one aware of the complex and profound understanding on which aiki-do actually rests.

This symbol expresses the movements of 'entrance and exit' in aiki-do.

The personal cipher of Master Andrew Nocquet who kindly contributed the photos of Master Ueshiba Morihei, under whom he studied personally.

Thoughts of Master Ueshiba Morihei

Do not look at the eyes of your opponent or your spirit will be lured into his eyes. Do not look at his sword or you will be killed by his sword. Do not look at him or your mind will be distracted. True budo is the culture of the attraction by which you draw the opponent towards you, as a complete entity. All I have to do is preserve this Way.

There is no opponent or enemy in true budo. True budo is at one with the universe which means being united with the centre of the universe. True budo is a labour of love. It involves giving life to all that exists and not killing or opposing one another. Love is the guardian angel of all things. Nothing exists without it. Aiki-do is the realization of love.

In aiki-do, we control the opponent's mind before confronting him. In other words, we draw him inside us. We progress in life with this strength of spirit and we strive to maintain a global view of the world.

We pray incessantly that the fight will not take place. For this reason, we strictly forbid aiki-do contests. Such contests still take place, however. The spirit of aiki-do is that of a loving attack and a peaceful reconciliation. With this aim in mind, we join and unite opponents with the ultimate power of love. We are able to purify others through love.

expression of this universe. To discover one's own identity and that of the universe, such is the fundamental experience which is the beginning of everything.

From this point of view, the opponent is once again a mere pretext, a sort of hallucination. Any resistance is just a vision, any obstacle is only there to be overcome and penetrated, just as universal energy traverses, unifies and transforms all things. This energy actually exists; it is breath and movement; it is time and progression; it can appear in many different forms but can only really be mastered and put to one's own use if the intention is pure.

In place of a sword, Ueshiba Morihei also says, aiki-do is a means to banish the devils with the sincerity of our breathing, in other words to transform the world from the demoniac spirit into a pure world. And again, 'the spirit of aiki-do is that of amorous attack and peaceful reconciliation'.

Only practice and almost total self-commitment enable one to discover the full meaning of these words; the highest degree of effectiveness is obtained at a sort of peak where the involuntary force becomes active. It is in fact obvious that the individual, freed of inner tension (fear, anguish, passion, etc.) becomes both the centre and the outlet of a fundamental energy – and that, from then on, this energy is expressed in many different ways, of which throwing one's opponent is, all things considered, simply one expression amongst many.

So, any true master can restore internal calm, heal the body, prevent certain illnesses, act on the body and soul as a whole and harmonize them.

In 1938, Master Ueshiba built a dojo and a Shinto temple at Iwama, 93 miles (150km) north of Tokyo, and began to teach aiki-do. Those who were fortunate enough to be admitted as pupils cultivated the land and served the master with total devotion.

The greatest masters of martial arts in Japan went to Iwama. Amongst them, Master Jigoro Kano, the founder of judo, who later sent Master Ueshiba a number of his pupils. To be allowed into the dojo merely as a spectator was in itself a great privilege. Any internal distraction or any form of behaviour which was not in keeping with the spirit of the dojo was noticed immediately by the master who stopped the session and made the visitor leave.

This way of life continued until the end of the last war, when the Americans restricted

The master Kisshomaru Ueshiba

the teaching of martial arts in all forms. Aiki-do was organized on new lines and in 1948 the Tokyo Aikikai opened. From then on, aiki-do was to spread throughout the world.

On 26 April 1969, Master Ueshiba Morihei died in Tokyo, aged 86, at the end of a long illness. The aiki-do taught by Master Ueshiba was aiki-do without form, an expression of the Void. 'Aiki-do', he would say, 'is not that which is expressed in movements but what comes well before the form is born, for aiki-do is a part of the psychical world of the Void.'

211

The world's great master in aiki-do is currently Kisshomaru Ueshiba. It is in these surroundings at Iwama that his father taught and founded the first aiki-do dojo, which has since become a place of worship.

The position of aiki-do today

It was predictable that when the great master died, and even during his lifetime, two trends were to become established. The first aimed at respecting the master's basic teaching, the second at adapting to the spirit of modern times by concentrating on technique and movements. Today, the two trends are causing an increasingly serious rift in aiki-do.

The technique point of view is popular by its vary nature. It conforms to the system of awarding grades or Dan, ratifies progress and enables the pupil to work in the knowledge that he is progressing according to predetermined standards.

By adapting a spiritual practice (which aiki-do essentially is) to a growing number of

followers, the inevitable thought comes naturally to mind. Quality and quantity: therein lies the question and the clue to understanding.

Those masters faithful to the fundamental teaching maintain that one can combine these two aspects, and that the choice will come naturally in the long run. Aiki-do is love. In this case, how can one mistrust others? Aiki-do is breath and respiration: how can one make the body supple and efficient without first calming body and mind? How can efficiency itself be surpassed if the very principle, by which the opponent is none other than oneself, is not understood?

It follows that aiki-do embraces such a strong sense of truth that an invisible thread must at any moment prompt the participant to say: 'Am I in the process of losing myself or finding myself?'

Is that not what the master meant when he said, 'There is neither form nor style in aiki-do; the movement of aiki-do is the movement of nature whose secret is profound and infinite?'

From two things, one thought emerges: either one acquires a state diploma, technique and reliability on one's reflexes being necessary and sufficient qualities, or not. If yes, what is there to say? If the answer is no, then the journey is not over. We know that in every long journey many set out and only a few arrive. Should that come as a surprise?

Aikikai is the only association in Japan which incorporates more than 700,000 devotees including 13,000 black belts and 56 university clubs. At present, aiki-do has about a million active followers in the world.

Master Ueshiba Morihei excelled in the art of staves which he considered, not as a separate technique, but as a stage in the teaching of aiki-do. Today, his son, Master Kisshomaru, confronts and throws several opponents in succession.

The practice of aiki-do

The practice of aiki-do of course reflects the personality of each master. However, we should retain a few basic principles of the teaching.

1. The prime object of aiki-do is not to learn to throw but to free the many psychic, organic and muscular obstacles common to modern man. The early stages (two months or more), are devoted to concentration on silence, to sensing the profound self through silence. Hence the study of positions and respiration.

2. Learning to free the force. To loosen all the tensions, joints and muscles, to bring about a harmonious circulation of the blood. The breath goes through the five branches of the body, the feet, hands and head. The hara is the result of this balance.

3. The being is relaxed and in this sense purified. At this stage, the force comes naturally. There is no longer any breathlessness nor any abrupt or broken movements; the body is freed; the movement comes spontaneously. It is at this point that the throws are introduced.

4. It is the vision and the perfect creation of the sphere, the vision of the circle. A new understanding of time and space emerges: time and distance no longer exist. It is said that speed begins, time is expressed in movements with a new swiftness and equality.

5. This is the moment of realization, of self-accomplishment. Every man becomes his own master.

Aiki-do is above all the art of opening one's mind, the opposite of the spirit of acquisition, of withdrawal, involving the combination of skill and technique. Essentially, it is the preparation of a state from which the relationship between oneself and the cosmic world enables movement to be expressed, not in an agressive form but primarily like a state of union and harmony between two partners. The throw is there to effect the completion of the movement and not to interrupt this movement with a crude break.

It is said that movement is expressed as a circle. In fact, this movement comes and goes, spreads out, turns back on itself in the image of a figure 8, ebbing and flowing, in other words expressing a constantly moving force which never stops.

It should be noted that in aiki-do the bo (staff) or the jo (stick) are employed, whilst taking on several armed opponents is used exclusively in training coaches.

215

Every aiki-do training session begins in meditation and bowing to the master.
Holds and throws by Master Kisshomaru Ueshiba. 1 – Armlock. 2 – Armlock for disarming an adversary. 3 – 4 – 5 – Pole thrusts.

Portrait of Master Funakoshi Gishin.

The Japanese Master Funakoshi Gishin who introduced karate to Japan in 1921, said
that the essence of karate is the art of being nonviolent.

Karate

Master Funakoshi Gishin

In 1922, the Japanese ministers of National Education invited an expert from Okinawa (Master Funakoshi Gishin) to give a karate demonstration. It was a great success and two years later Keio university founded Japan's first karate dojo. The great master of judo himself, Jigoro Kano, expressed a wish to learn karate. Under the direction of Master Funakoshi, followed in 1930 by another great master from Okinawa, Master Mabuni, karate over the years became extremely popular throughout Japan.

Bodhidharma and the Shaolin school

It seems that between 502 and 550 an Indian monk, Bodhidharma (Daruma in Japanese, Ta-mo in Chinese), arrived in China. He was about 60. With the powers he appeared to possess, he made an extraordinary impression. However, Bodhidharma went into meditation surrounded by many disciples. After nine years of leading an ascetic life, he noticed that his disciples who were weak and thin through deprivation formed a sorry sight.

So, he taught them physical exercises combined with breathing, called *ta-ch'uan* (or *da quan*). Part of this teaching was formed into a 'Treatise on Limbering up the Joints' and a 'Treatise on Limbering up the Bones'.

Bodhidharma is then said to have taught in a famous monastery called Shaolin, founded in 495 in the Henan district of northern China. For centuries, the Shaolin temple was in fact the centre for over 400 varieties of Chinese boxing. Here, it is understood that the word 'boxing' has a particular meaning embracing even the very slow gentle movements like *t'ai-chi* (or *taiji quan*).

During the Sung dynasty, a monk named Shang San-feng modified and perfected the forms used and, in contrast to the *external method* used until then, he introduced the *internal method,* so defining their differences. The external method regularizes respiration, exercises the bones and the muscles, teaches the art of attack and defence, the unity of the harsh and the gentle forces. The internal method comprises the training of bones and muscles, facing the attack calmly, and its object is to overcome the enemy the moment he attacks.

If Bodhidharma is surrounded by a legendary halo, it is certain that the Shaolin school (even if it was not the only one) played a decisive role in the knowledge of the art of fighting or exercise with bare hands.

As the tradition of secrecy was until recent times absolute as far as the Chinese masters were concerned, it is difficult to know how it was handed down. Even in Okinawa, there is no written evidence of karate or its allied forms such as *te* before the writings of Master Funakoshi himself. Numerous Japanese schools claim to practise the teaching of the Shaolin temple (called Shorin in Japanese) but they probably have little in common with this school.

Okinawa and te, or art of empty hands

Meetings and exchanges between Japanese and Chinese masters have always taken place. From Master Higaonna, whose pupil Funakoshi was, to Funakoshi himself, the subtle bond with China was ever present throughout these exchanges.

Note that Japanese masters always speak of Chinese masters with the greatest respect. Even today, such meetings sometimes take place and are a revelation making one aware of unsuspected knowledge and powers.

It is certain in any case that the Chinese masters took the secrets of their art to Okinawa. In fact, in the 17th century, the Japanese invaded the island and gradually all

fighting weapons were prohibited and confiscated. Chinese methods of combat were then adapted under the name okinawa-te or simply te meaning 'hands'.

In 1903, the Japanese, surprised at the physical performance of young conscripts during te practice, authorized its teaching in school. The name karate-jutsu replaced the word 'te'. Karate-jutsu, taken from Chinese ideograms meant 'art of the hands' in Chinese.

In 1932, the emergence of a new style of karate in Japan meant another name: the Chinese ideogram 'Kara' meaning China was replaced by an ideogram pronounced the same way but meaning 'empty'. So, modern karate or 'art of empty hands' was born and Master Funakoshi was the first to determine its synthesis. In fact, he took his inspiration from all the martial arts connected with karate: okinawa-te, kempo, t'ai-chi, etc. He studied all these methods and devoted a long lifetime (he died when he was 83) to making them known.

The Shorenji-kempo school shelters Buddhist monks who practise karate as a complement to meditation. As well as using the fists, their technique involves leaps and throws.

Shorenji (leaps and throws).

Master Nakano, assistant head of the Shorenji-kempo, teaching his pupils how to leap up and strike someone's face with the sole of their foot. He himself can jump higher than two yards. At present, there are about 300,000 people who practise this style of karate in Japan.

Shotokan karate

Within Master Funakoshi Gishin's Shotokan school of karate, different schools appeared, some seeking technical impact and competency above all (Masters Nakayama, Kase and Nishiyama) and others putting the accent on the mental aspect of karate (Masters Oshima, Harda, Okuyama and Egami).

Even today, the Shotokan school has the greatest number of supporters in Japan (one third of the total) and in Europe. While respecting tradition, Shotokan karate has concentrated on etiquette, vitality, the sporting aspect and competition. Shotokan etiquette can be found in the giri, ninjo and bushido notions.

The giri notion of Confucian origin expresses respect for the master, the ancestors and tradition. It is the sense of duty or gratitude towards the man responsible for one's education.

Ninjo expresses the humanitarian aspect of Buddhism, compassion towards others which attenuates and counterbalances the violent, rough side of budo: it is magnanimity.

This Shotokan school has produced the most formidable karate champions in recent years; the quality of their training, their acute fighting sense, their exemplary conduct, have enabled them to win all the main international competitions.

The Shotokan attitude to shiwari or 'the break': it is a vital test of competency at a certain level but one would be wrong to stop there. It helps above all to develop the kime, that is to say the maximum amount of concentration on a specific spot at a given time. The blow does not stop at the plank but continues beyond it.

Control of respiration is defined as: 'Finding the dead time in movement and movement in the dead time', which constitutes the whole essence of a contest.

Respiration evolves in two cycles: inhaling and exhaling, with the possibility of holding one's breath after inhaling. Inhaling and holding one's breath relate to contraction, exhaling to relaxation. Between the two cycles, i.e. after exhaling and before inhaling, there is a dead time. One must sense the opponent's dead time, however insignificant, in order to launch an attack.

It is the combined use of physical and psychological principles which forms the basis of karate, according to Master Nishiyama. One must, he says, have a mind as calm as a millpond (*mizu-no-kokoro*).

As for Master Nakayama, his favourite kata is meikyo: apparently the legendary origin of this kata was evocative of the dance the gods performed in order to make the Sun Goddess Amaterasu come out of the cave where she was hiding.

This kata is the best example of the deep relationship between karate and the Japanese spirit.

Some of Master Nakayama's pupils

(*below*) A young karateka breaking planks with his foot (shiwari) while uttering the kiai.
Practice leap.

above) Master Nakayama Masatoshi (9th Dan) born in 1913, was a pupil of Master Gishin Funakoshi.
He is seen here in his dojo in Tokyo performing a movement in front of his pupils.
He is a renowned exponent of Shotokan karate.

below left) A pupil executes a practice kick.

(*below right*) Breaking a plank with the fist.
The wrist joints can be used for attack or defence (a) back of the wrist or kakuto, (b) hand folded as tightly as possible facing upwards or teisho, (c) wrist folded back to expose the base of the thumb or keito, (d) using the edge of the hand or seiryuto.

Master Yamaguchi and the Goju-Ryu

Around 1931, Yamaguchi Gogen met, in Tokyo, Master Miyagi, founder of the Goju-Ryu. Together, they developed their understanding of karate, which he had studied for several years. When Miyagi died in 1952, Yamaguchi succeeded him and became master of the Gojo-Ryu, which since then has greatly expanded, especially in the United States where his three sons teach.

Renowned throughout the world for his long hair and feline expression giving him his nickname 'The Cat', Master Yamaguchi enjoyed practising karate and meditation. He spent long periods out of doors and practised the spectacular form of meditation sitting at the foot of a waterfall cascading on to the top of his head.

The Goju-Ryu technique combines strength (go) and gentleness (ju). Respiration synchronized with movements or figures plays an important part. (Ibuki and development of the kokyu). The kata (or pre-determined figures) are performed slowly and the attacks are made using strength if the opponent attacks the subtle way and subtly if the opponent uses strength.

This hard and realistic method attempts to combine expressiveness and strength. Hence short or weak movements. In fact, everything hangs on the rhythms of contractions and relaxations.

The Goju-Ryu method has its origins in Okinawa where Master Higaonna taught it to Miyagi but, since then, Master Yamaguchi has influenced it with his powerful personality. Imbued with a strong religious sentiment, he actually founded the Karate-Shinto, a sort of syncretic ryu where those assimilated in the principles of Zen, karate, yoga and Shinto gathered.

During his long stays in the mountains where he lived alone, he subjected himself to ascetic exercises and chastening. He worshipped the kami and the forces of nature. His physical and mental training was aimed at discovering original purity and the state of enlightenment.

One of the masters' favourite practices is to meditate beneath a waterfall. The water falling on the crown of the head creates a state which is particularly favourable to internal awakening. It is also an ancient rite of Shamanic origin the object of which is to draw Power from the waterfall.

In the Gojo-Ryu, respiration plays a decisive role. Breathing starts in the hara, rises and makes the body vibrate. It is a deep sonorous breathing from the stomach.

The master performing a kata.

Kihon: basic training. Devotees train by punching the air while running (similar training for kicking). While running, the karateka utters the kiai.

Two of the master's teaching methods are called sanchin and tensho.

Sanchin more often than not is performed stripped to the waist while breathing deeply and sonorously from the stomach – changes in posture called sanchi-dachi are very slight.

Tensho is the same as zazen (or nonmeditation in a sitting position). The mind–body union is achieved by respiration control. The exercise is performed in a gentle and relaxed way.

Shotokai karate and Master Egami

Master Egami was director of the Shotokai school in Tokyo, a school where entry is difficult and open to those seeking above all a spiritual development in karate. Karate is becoming much more of an art than an exercise, and as such can be interpreted in different ways by the masters. Variations result, some good, some bad, all liable to evolve in the continuing progression.

An example of this is the case of one of Master Egami's pupils: Master Aoki who interprets karate as a method of searching rather than the outcome of a technique.

The breaking of planks as a demonstration of its effectiveness holds no interest for this master. 'One fights men, not trees', he says. The first is closed in such a way that the second finger, although folded in, stands out. The blow's penetration is therefore more profound and the striking power concentrated on one spot.

The object of the training is to reach a second level of performance. Quite often it take place on a beach of deep sand which makes the movements more difficult. In fact, the training is intended to surpass pure physical and muscular strength. It is impor-

tant to exhaust one's physical strength, to relax the body and make it supple, before the second level of energy can come into play.

At the first level, the blow strikes an adversary, a plank or an obstacle and stops at this obstacle. At the second level, a new kind of energy is active: kime, that is a physical force which goes beyond the straightforward blow, a force which penetrates the obstacle and keeps going.

Both voluntary action and reflex action have to be surpassed, in order to achieve total spontaneity. As in the art of loosing the arrow, the instinctive trigger acts instantaneously and shoots, once all tenseness has been eliminated or controlled.

According to Master Egami: 'The only secret is to practise seriously with perseverance, in order to attain the state of mushin (non-ego) which opens the doors of the hara to consciousness.'

The state of non-ego is the opportunity to be in harmony with nature, to work in accordance with it and to absorb oneself totally in it. This type of karate or karate-do seeks the unity of body and mind through understanding and assimilating the harmonics of the universe.

Master Egami expressed this unity as *hei-ho*.

'When I began to understand the hei-ho notion, I trembled with immense pleasure', he said. 'Hei-ho is the art of living once one has transcended the idea of living and dying – it is therefore the art of study and being a part of the true life.'

The opponent is master

In the normal state of life, everything is opposed. Fundamental nature on the other hand represents unity. To attain this unity means surpassing the visible evidence, so that the opponent becomes the master: he is like a part of oneself which one confronts, not in order to destroy it, but to be united with it.

Rules for use in practice

— Receive and escort your opponent like a distinguished guest.
— Discover true love through training.

Three men practising with the bokken or wooden sword.

Exercise intended to produce freedom of respiration and collective euphoria.

— Discover movement in the dead time and the dead time in movement.

— Discover the immensity of the cosmos within the scope of man.

Master Aoki practises respiration from the hara (or stomach) synchronized with certain sounds corresponding to the five vowels in Japanese.

Working with the bokken (or wooden sword): rending the air a thousand times or more with the bokken is simply a prelude to an exercise intended to develop the sixth sense or sense of telepathic apperception.

Three pupils stand one behind the other, a distance apart, with their eyes closed and wooden swords held in the seigan position

(half-guard). The first of the three must anticipate the intention of the other two to launch an attack and forestall it by counterattacking. This exercise can be explained scientifically as the order to attack is transmitted from the brain to the nerve centres by waves; with the right training and in a state of deep concentration, it becomes possible to intercept these waves. He who can read his opponent's intentions in this way, is ahead of him in time. Perfection demands direct action, not premeditated but spontaneous, released by intuition, of which only the great masters who have mastered and even transcended their art are capable.

The three great schools

Master Funakoshi's method of teaching, known as *Shotokan* (1922), is today the best known in France and Japan.

Several years later, in 1930, Master Miyagi Chojun, leader of the Nahate ryu, introduced the *goju-ryu* which is today taught by Master Yamaguchi (in Japan) and his three sons (in the United States).

A third master helped to found Japanese karate: Mabuni Kenwa, founder of the Shito-Ryu in 1926.

Within these great schools, there are different trends in style. Proper Japanese karate is established in the Wado-Ryu (tradition of the Way of Peace). In a simple effective style based on natural movements, the Wado-Ryu embraces a large number of experts settled in Europe.

In addition, we should mention the Kyokushinkai directed by Oyama Masutatsu, and the Shorenji-Kempo which combines karate with Buddhist meditation.

The Japanese Karate Association was founded in 1948. The various karate schools and institutions in the United States are governed by the rules of the United Karate Federation, founded in 1965.

Resistance to pain.

A karateka must be master of himself under all circumstances. For this reason, Master Shiokawa's pupils undergo practice in withstanding pain: kicks in the stomach by the master, karate blows on different parts of the body – arms, legs, chest, etc. During these exercises, the pupil must keep his self-control and a 'mind like the surface of water', calm as a millpond.

There are three basic movements to remember:
1. Oi-tsuki (and gyaku-tsuki).
2. Mae-geri: attack with the foot.
3. Mawashi-geri: circular kick.

1. Oi-tsuki is attacking with the fist – essential to the study of karate.
2. Mae-geri, or attack with the foot (right or left) – striking out sideways or forwards, either with the heel or with the sole of the foot.
3. Yoko-geri (ki-hon): circular kick.

Then all the ancillary variations such as the backwards kick.

Kicking practice (mae-geri).

Karate's natural weapons

1, 4 – Direct hit: using the front part of the fist but only the knuckles of the second and third metacarpal bones and not the whole surface (kento)
2 – Hammer first blow
3 – Punch using all the fingers
5 – Hammer thumb blow
6 – Reverse thrust
7, 8 – One finger punch
9, 10 – Clenched fist punch
11 – Edge of hand chop
12 – Edge of thumb chop
13 – Blow with the back of the hand
14 – Blow with the palm of the hand
15 – Fingertips thrust
16 – One finger thrust
17 – Two finger thrust
18 – Cupped hands blow
19 – 'Eagle's beak' blow
20 – Blow with the base of the palm
21 – Blow with the top of the wrist
22 – Blow with the base of the hand's edge
23 – Blow with the top edge of the wrist
24 – The elbow
25 – One can block more effectively with the fleshy part of the arm, either side of the elbow
26 – Inside edge, thumb side
27 – Outside edge, little finger side
28 – Ball of the foot
29 – Sole of the foot
30 – The heel
31 – Top of the foot
32 – Points of the toes
33 – Side of the foot
34 – The knee

The drawings 1 to 34 are taken from Roland Habersetzer's book: *Karate*, pages 86, 88, 92, published (in French) by Marabout.

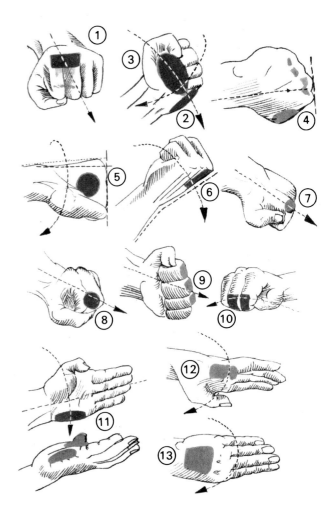

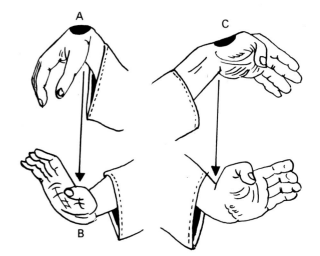

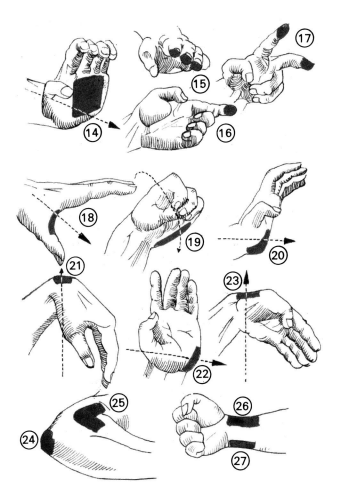

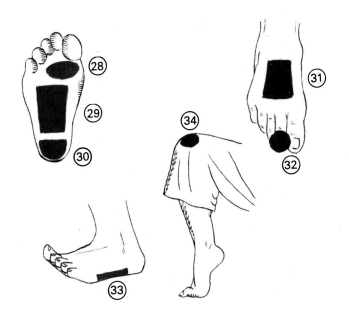

Target areas
in karate

EIDO ZUKI   HASAMI ZUKI   TETSUI UCHI   YOKO HIJI ATE   MAE HIJI ATE   USHIRO HIJI ATE

Judo

Portrait of Master Kano Jigoro.

Judo or the Way of flexibility

In the literal sense, judo means 'Way of flexibility' and although popularized in 1882, there is evidence of its ancient noble connections.

If suddenly disarmed, how could a samurai contend with his enemy's sword using only his hands and feet? In Japan, numerous schools strove for centuries to answer this question by studying all sorts of techniques in the utmost secrecy. So much so that a wide variety of names was given to these techniques: yawara, wajutsu, kogusoku, kumiuchi, kempo, hakuda, shubaku, etc.

Of judo's many possible forerunners, let us recall the story of a Nagasaki doctor, Akyiama Shinobu, who is said to have learnt, while in China, three hakuda techniques and 28 methods of kuappo, or ways of reviving a person who appears dead.

As his techniques met with little success, Akyiama buried himself in deep meditation for 100 days. The snow fell heavily and beneath its weight many trees suffered broken branches. However, Akyiama noticed a willow which was so pliable that the snow could not accumulate on it. This made such an impression on him that he invented 300 jujutsu movements, thus founding the Yoshin-Ryu (or tradition of the Heart of Willow).

Judo has emerged from several martial arts ryu. (The term judo itself was used as early as the Tokugawa period by the Jikishin Ryu).

However, Master Tsunetoshi Iikubu, who taught Kano Jigoro the founder of kodokan judo, joined the jujutsu Kito Ryu.

This ryu is based on the teaching of two secret books: *Hontai* and *Seiko,* handed down by the Bonze Takuan-Zenshi. The school's name, Ki-To, itself expresses the positive form (ki = to raise up) and the negative form (to = to strike down). The principles of judo are therein explained.

One must win with compliance, by knowing how to make use of the opposing strength while conserving one's own, a virtually impossible aim.

Hontai signifies the wisdom gained by mastering the body with the mind. This wisdom, according to the monk Takuan, must reflect the immobile spirit which is not in any one place. Directing one's thoughts to some point, such as the opponent's weapon during a fight, a part of the body in a meditation exercise, etc., reduces one's concentration, narrows the mind and dilutes one's faculties of open and intuitive perception; consequently one's ability to retaliate is also weakened.

Randori: free exercise and free thought

Not concentrating on any one thing also means freeing oneself of all the thoughts that preoccupy man: ego, passion and any kind of fixation. 'When the mind is nowhere in particular', said Takuan, 'it is called spirit without thought. To concentrate one's mind on something is called spirit with thought.' Therefore, the mind must be active without concentrating on any one thing.

In judo, this mental attitude is found in randori, meaning 'free exercise', which creates all the conditions of a real fight. Kano Jigoro said: 'The two partners must always be on the alert to try to discover the opponent's weaknesses by being ready to attack as soon as the opportunity arises.'

This state of alertness means being aware of all our faculties and is not a state of mental analysis preparatory to making the riposte. In such a case, there is a dead time, a pause (called bonno – that is to say, a 'disturbing passion'). On the other hand, a calm clear mind will not, it is said, allow a hair's breadth to come between the attack and the riposte – and this sudden swiftness is in itself the art of using the opponent's strength to one's own advantage, or of making use of the opposing force without having to use one's own.

The highest degree of competency, if that is the desired goal, is brought about by the maximum amount of serenity. In judo, the science of counterthrows or go no sen means the frame of mind which ensures victory. J. L. Jazarin said: 'Quicker than go no sen, the art of sen no sen means not waiting for the attack to be decided. It counters it, it begins at the same moment as the attack. The attempt to attack is anticipated and instantaneously countered.'[1]

The freedom of spirit of a good Judoka is like a polished mirror, free to reflect and to face up to any possible change. This state of mind and such physical action are known as 'sei' or tranquility and 'do' or action, or sometimes 'ju' and 'go' meaning delicacy and firmness, or 'in' and 'yo' – negative and positive, etc.

Beyond energy itself

However, if Kano Jigoro said that: 'The skilful use and application of force and energy are the essential elements of judo', he also added: 'The best expression of energy is to achieve the best possible result from the least possible force.'

The very essence of judo lies in 'ju' (or yawara) implying delicacy. Delicacy and gentleness, used to negate the opponent's strength without unnecessary effort, are an even more enviable finality which only the great masters possess. It is the 'power of life' and continual progression which is active and which, observing the law of movement, works on movement from within and not on the opposing force.

[1] *The Spirit of Judo,* published (in French) by Le Pavillon, page 80.

The centre of gravity and the laws of movement

As far as the Japanese are concerned, the centre of balance or the centre of gravity in the body is the point which relates man to the earth, to nature, to the cosmos, and is therefore man's actual nucleus, in physical as well as psychical terms.

The principle of judo could be depicted as a circle expressing movement in space and by a point in the centre of the circle expressing the centre or axis of gravity.

Life is progression; so long as man maintains his physical centre of gravity he is master of all his faculties; when he loses it, he enters a state of instability and inferiority. Movement acts on the centre of gravity (symbol of permanency and durability) and by adjusting it he creates a progression. When Kano Jigoro said: 'The object of judo is to understand and demonstrate swiftly the living laws of movement', it was an invitation which went far beyond the concern for maximum competency, one imagines. Beyond judo, one should understand the law of life itself.

In this sense, all the martial arts seek the balance of the centre of gravity; concentration of the hara as we know lies in psychical and physical harmony.

Free movement

Concern for effectiveness kills effectiveness for, in the end, it is not always possible to calculate movement. Judo reflects life, the law of accident or the unexpected; the blow which, in a sudden loss of balance, launches the body on a painful fall.

That is why judo teaches free attack (sutemi) expressing total self-commitment as if one's life was being sacrificed, just as it teaches free falling without fear or tension which in themselves cause accidents and fractures.

So, knowing how to fall is a prime art of judo. To respond with suppleness to the opponent's movement and to help the movement along is also what gives randori its rhythm and respiration. Given the choice of two opponents locked together, each trying to be the strongest, or two opponents who fall with the movement, progress will be very much faster in the second case.

Hence the danger of competitions. J. L. Jazarin said that as a sport, judo is dangerous both for the judoka and for judo itself.[1]

'In fact, the partisan spirit, passion for the game, pride – be it collective, national, regional, urban, or club – not to mention the material interest attached to the titles except in passing, all these emotional feelings break out and drown the spirit of justice and truth, and the sense of chivalry, even in the best of people.

The partner becomes the opponent, then the enemy, the man to be beaten by any means. Trickery and deception . . . all is permissible. The aim is to win and to win at all costs, no matter how, and above all, not to lose. Stopping or preventing the other from functioning when one is not the stronger of the two, all goes to make bad judo which is no longer judo at all.

Master Kano Jigoro, who did not escape these dangers, was opposed to public competions and championships.

The five oaths of judo

When judo was first created, all the judokas in training at the kodokan put the seal of blood to the open register before declaring the following five oaths:
1. Once admitted to the kodokan, I shall not stop my study of judo without good reason.
2. I shall not dishonour the dojo.
3. I shall not tell or show the secrets I have been taught to anyone, without authorization.
4. I shall not teach judo without authorization.
5. First as a pupil, later as a teacher, I shall always obey the rules of the dojo.

'Judo seen as a means of attack or defence can only be one of these', said Kano Jigoro. In the wider sense, judo is primarily an art or philosophy of life, applied not only to the development of intellectual and moral strength, but also to food, society life, business, etc.
[1] As Master Kano pointed out: 'The study of the principle in general terms is more important than the simple practice of ju-jutsu.'

[1] *Judo, School of Life* by J. L. Jazarin, published (in French) by Le Pavillon, p. 137.

Portrait of Master Kano Jigoro in his garden with his wife.

Dix-Septième année. — N° 879.   Huit pages : CINQ centimes   Dimanche 10 Décembre 1905.

Le Petit Parisien

SUPPLÉMENT LITTÉRAIRE ILLUSTRÉ

TOUS LES JOURS
Le Petit Parisien
(Six pages)
5 centimes
—
CHAQUE SEMAINE
LE SUPPLÉMENT LITTÉRAIRE
5 centimes

DIRECTION : 18, rue d'Enghien (10e), PARIS

ABONNEMENTS

PARIS ET DÉPARTEMENTS :
12 mois, 4 fr. 50. 6 mois, 2 fr. 25
UNION POSTALE :
12 mois, 5 fr 50. 6 mois, 3 fr.

UNE SÉANCE DE JIU-JITSU

Jujutsu and judo

The following are the basic rules of judo and jujutsu.

As the fundamental principle of judo is to throw one's opponent, using the minimum amount of force, in order to achieve this result, one must:

1. First of all assess and employ the opponent's forces.
2. Avoid his attacks.
3. During the fight, draw him into an unfavourable position while maintaining one's own good posture.
4. At the moment of attack, aim for his weakest point.
5. Use the lever technique to bring him down.
6. To hold him down, once thrown, immobilize the joints, select the points where pressure causes pain (ju-jutsu only).
7. In some attacks, try to make him lose consciousness by means of knocks or blows to certain parts of the body (ju-jutsu only).

Judo comprises three categories of exercises:

1. *Atemi-waza,* art of causing the opponent to faint, or killing him.
2. *Kuatsu,* art of reviving an opponent who is apparently dead.
3. Throws, locks and everything relating to defence: twisting the limbs, immobilizing the joints.

And free exercise.

Kano Jigoro: founder of judo

However, a man called Kano Jigoro formulated a new concept called judo from the old techniques of jujutsu.

Born in 1860, Kano Jigoro, like Ueshiba Morihei, had a weak constitution. In his twentieth year he learnt jujutsu, convinced of the need to train his body and mind. Five years later, the sickly young man who often came off worst in student brawls, had become a strong man and master of himself. He continued to study and progressively perfected his own technique to which he gave the name kodokan-judo (kodokan: ryu for studying the Way, and judo, Way of flexibility).

Kano Jigoro (1860-1938), founder of the kodokan, in his judo suit.

'Jujutsu ryu,' wrote Kano Jigoro, 'employed dangerous practices such as throwing by quite incorrect methods or by roughly applying torsion to the limbs.'

Jujutsu did not enjoy a good reputation in view of the fact that all sorts of undesirable people practised it at the expense of others. That is why Kano adopted the name judo. In 1882, with just nine pupils, he opened his first judo school. When he died in 1938 – at the age of 78 – judo already had over 100,000 black belts to its name.

Mental training in judo can take the form of the kata method or the randori method, but preferably the latter. The attitude of mind when seeking means of attack is such that it tends to make the pupil frank and attentive, wise and thoughtful in all his actions. At the same time, he is trained to take quick decisions for, if prompt action is not taken, the opportunity for attack or defence is always missed.

Furthermore, in randori, neither partner can tell what his opponent will do, such that each must always be prepared to counter any sudden attack attempted by the other. Once he is used to this mental attitude, man acquires a high level of self-control. By exercising one's power of attention and observation in the training room, this power, so useful in everyday life, develops naturally.

Breaking balance, leg and arm movements.

 1

 2

 4

 5

 8

 9

 10

 12

 13

 14

Randori

This involves the acts of throwing, choking, and holding the opponent down. The two opponents can use any method provided they do not hurt each other and respect the rules of judo in terms of etiquette.

Kata

Kata – the word literally means 'form' – is a strict system of prearranged exercises including acts of hitting, chopping, kicking, punching, etc., according to the rules by which each contestant knows in advance what his opponent will do. Training in such acts is given in kata but not in randori because if they were used in randori people could frequently get hurt, whilst during kata teaching one cannot be injured because all the actions of attack and defence are prearranged.

That is why it is customary to say that kata not only represents the grammar of judo but also its form and rule of conduct. However, some kata such as itsutsu-no-kata (kata of the five principles) are references to the great forces of nature and are inspired by the interaction, flowering, cohesion and logic of these forces.

The *koshiki-no-kata* was Master Kano Jigoro's favourite kata: he practised and studied it continually, saying that it constituted the very essence of judo. The names given to some of his movements are reminiscent of his spirit and his research. In the form *omote:* (1) tai (body); (2) yume-no-uchi (in the mind); (3) ryoku-hi (heki) (control of energy); (4) mizu-guruma (the wheel of running water); (5) mizu-nagare (the water running in the stream); . . . (13) yu-dachi (evening storm in summer).

In the form *ura:* (3) mizu-iri (letting the water flow); (4) kyu-setsu (the weight of the snow); (5) saka-otoshi (fall on the slope); (6) yuki-ore (the snow breaks the branch); (7) iwa-nami (waves against the rocks).

It could be thought that these different designations are only of interest to the Japanese poetic spirit – far from it, each describes literally the form of the movement and the form of energy applied.

'The *ju no kata* (flexible forms) is full of instructions for continuity of movement,

The four main principles of learning judo.

1. Kata study to ensure accuracy in balance and movement.
2. Uchi-komi or constant practice of a movement previously studied in kata training.
3. Experiment in movement by randori.
4. Shiai = the contest: competency finally put to the test.

Here are some examples of movements using different forms of breakfalls, as well as ground work (which also involves breaking balance). At one time, in order to become a 1st Dan, one had to perform randori-no-kata, which was an interrupted demonstration of nage-no-kata (throwing kata) and katame no kata (ground movements in kata) for judo is equally divided between ground work and movements performed standing up.

1. Breakfalls, movements of arms and legs Hiza-guruma: Note that tori (the active partner) breaks his opponent's balance on the right leg. The fall is caused by locking the knee and uke's dynamic energy with the help of tori. (photos 1, 2 and 3)

Harai goshi: Movement using the hip as a pivot enabling the body to rotate, making a clean sweep. (4, 5, 6, and 7)

Tai-otoshi: Breaking balance on the right or left side; accentuating this unbalance and blocking the right foot with the right leg. (8, 9, 10 and 11)

Uki-waza: Different sutemi – an example of breaking balance using the 'body sacrifice' method. (12, 13 and 14)

Yoko-wakare: Body sacrifice. (15)

logic in actions and variations in breakfalls. It is performed without a break between the figures – there are no breakfalls. Before the last war, it was compulsory in Japan, from 3rd Dan onwards, and Master Kano Jigoro would make his followers practise it before and after each training session. For, apart from the research and teaching contained in it, if performed before and after randori, it reminds one of the sense of gentleness and of true judo, while limbering up the body and mind.'[1]

[1]*Judo, School of Life,* J. L. Jazarin, published (in French) by Le Pavillon, p. 161.

2. Immobilization holds

Kuzure kami shiho gatame: Immobilization hold and lateral variations on immobilizing the top half of the body.

Kuzure kesa gatame: Immobilizing the head (*kuzure variation*).

3. Cross Hold
Jugi-gatame: Crossed arm lock.

4. Strangle hold
Kata-ha-jime: Single wing stranglehold (from *jime* meaning strangle).

Here, the judokas are Christian Cervenansky (4th Dan) and Louis Renelleau (5th Dan).

Sumo

Being an exclusive art, sumo has not been popularized. It has remained a competitive art. In Japan there are, at the most, 50 great sumotori who compete in tournaments. But, whereas in judo or karate championships there are always a few spare places, sumo contests arouse immense excitement and all the places are snatched up long in advance.

During sumo tournaments, each contest is transmitted live on television. As the hour of the big fights draws near, in all the dojo and in the kodokan in Tokyo, the great champions of martial arts gather in front of television sets to watch these important contests. A great sumo champion is in fact virtually unconquerable. He therefore considers himself to rank above all the other devotees of martial arts and, as a result, remains fiercely independent.

Sumo is of ancient origin and, both in former times and today, the contests were between giants. Many sumotori weighed over 265lb (120kg) and were taller than 6ft 8in (2.10m). But it was not until about 724 that an edict forbad the killing of a sumotori who had fallen to the ground. Until then he would have been trampled to death. After that, sumo became a method of training samurai in man to man combat. At the same time, the development of sumo was related to Shinto religious spirit, so that even today, the little Shinto altar is always present in sumo dojo.

A sumo fight is in itself relatively short, lasting a few minutes at most. It involves throwing the opponent outside a holy circle. So, the attack is extremely swift and violent. Beforehand, the two heavyweights balance like great bears, first on one foot, then on the other, with their legs well apart. Then they crouch and bow to each other. In competitions, the referee waits until both men are breathing regularly before letting them fight. This gives rise to unimaginable suspense because neither the sumotori nor the spectators know at what precise moment the signal will be given to begin. Sometimes in grand championships the start can be put off up to ten times.

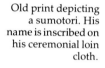

Old print depicting a sumotori. His name is inscribed on his ceremonial loin cloth.

Taiho, the greatest sumo champion of all times, during the ceremony preceding the fight. After clapping his hands, he stretches them out with open palms to signify that he has no weapons and that the fight will be a fair one. Then he lifts a leg and stamps to expel the evil spirits.

Such suspense which Westerners would find hard to bear, has its purpose. Here, the impact of attack is carried to its highest degree of perfection. Two sudden and immense forces must confront each other and conquer in a flash. Each contestant therefore tries to stabilize his physical and mental forces to the utmost, as well as his breathing and tension-free frame of mind from whence the essential force will surge.

This method of quickly gathering together all one's faculties is known as *tachi-ai*. The great champion, Taiho, who is possibly the greatest sumo fighter of all times, would literally smash his opponents out of the dojo. He won 31 championships consecutively. At the age of 19, he became the greatest champion (or yokozuna) ever known. He was 5ft 10in (1.87m) tall and weighed 14 stone (149kg). Today, Taiho has retired unconquered and is a sumo coach.

There are more than 800 sumo fighters in Japan. Recruited at a very early age – 12 or 13 – the young man who embarks on a career of sumotori enters a ryu but also undertakes a discipline which will become the sole purpose of his life until he retires.

The training is arduous and the goal which will guarantee fame and fortune a distant one – the title of great champion is almost unattainable. In sumo's entire history, there have only been 52 yokozuna.

The severe training lasts four hours a day. To learn to push violently shoulder to shoulder, hand to hand, to strive for speed, to breathe, to perfect even the most simple movements, are just some aspects of a training which is extremely complex.

Like judoka, sumotori learn to use the opponent's force. However, the sumotori's strength and technical competency is such that only a sumotori can withstand the attack of another sumotori.

The great champion Sadano Yama.

Here he is executing the doyo-iri, that is to say a ceremony of Shinto character in which the great champion asks the gods to help him win. Only the great champion has the right to wear a holy rope, similar to the Shinto shimenawa.

The art of grabbing the opponent by the belt and throwing him out of the circle.

A young sumo champion has thrown his opponent to the ground; other sumotori rush forward to fight with him.

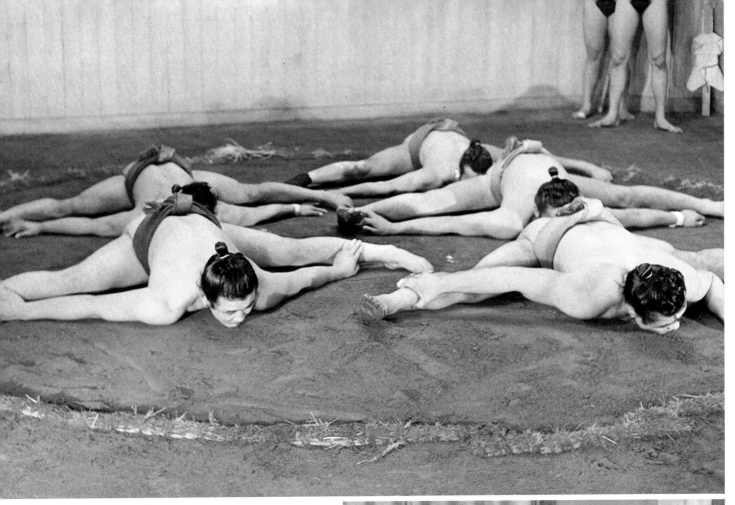

Young sumotori during a limbering up exercise: they are doing the splits sideways while keeping their chin on the ground, a feat which few dancers, even experienced ones, are able to accomplish.

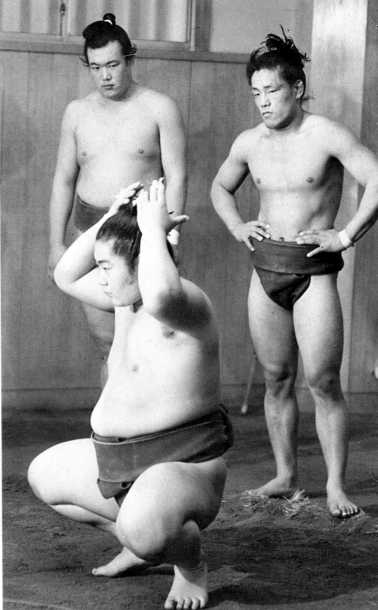

Sumo or 'fight with bare hands' is the most traditional of all Japanese martial arts. There are only about 50 great sumotori in Japan: some weigh more than 315lbs (150kg) and can measure nearly 6ft 2in (2m). A sumo fight is relatively short, lasting a few minutes at most. It consists of throwing the adversary out of a small circle marked out on the ground. The attack is therefore extremely swift and violent.

The great champion Kashiwado entering the dojo.

He is assisted by two high-ranking sumotori. One carries the sword, symbol of his dignity. On the left, the referee (or gyoji) wearing a samurai ceremonial kimono which has not changed in 600 years. The great champion claps his hands to attract the gods' attention, according to the Shinto rite.

A popular poster. Samurai practising sumo. True sumotori learn how to withdraw their testicles before a fight as a precautionary measure.

250

Entrance of the maki-uchi or group of champions. They all wear sumptuous loin-cloths (keshomawashi) donated by their supporters.

The origin of sumo is very old and merges with the origin of Japan itself. However, it was not until the 16th century that the present rules were adopted. That was when the professional sumotori appeared, professional in the sense that they did not work and were supported by the lords. However, military applications of sumo continued to be studied by the samurai, so that sumo could be regarded as one of the bases of jujutsu and judo. Today, sumo has reached a highly refined level. As an exclusive art, it is still confined to a small élite who contend for the title. A great sumo champion regards his art as being superior to all the other martial arts.

The art of techniques

Japanese martial techniques are numerous, due to the fact that Japanese feudalism continued until the middle of the last century (300 years longer than in Europe). In spite of the introduction of fire arms and although the samurai were at first reluctant to use them, their proliferation sparked off a renewed interest in traditional martial techniques. It is obvious that the use of fire arms destroyed the Way of the samurai which identified with noble weapons. The rejection and contempt of these fire arms on the part of some old-fashioned people was so strongly felt that in 1877 Saigo Takamori's samurai, in revolt against the emperor, opposed the guns of the newly formed people's army with only their samurai swords – choosing to die in this way rather than adapt to modern times.

Moreover, the Japanese spirit, prodigiously inclined to get to the depth of the matter as soon as it is a question of combining the practical with the spiritual, effectiveness with the Way, has not missed the opportunity to add each weapon or each warlike technique to the established methods, rules and concepts which have been developed in depth.

For example, there is the martial Way of swimming which, at one time, was only taught to samurai. It is a sort of standing up method enabling a warrior, weighed down by his arms and armour, to cross a river against all odds.

The famous tessen or iron fan was used, a weapon wielded with surprising skill.

Tantojutsu or dagger fencing demanded the talents of a magician: the knife passing from one hand to the other, in front, behind the back, turning in the hand so quickly that one could not follow it with the eye, nor know when to expect an attack.

There was also a wide range of long arms (nagai-mono) and short arms (mi-jikai-mono), which were not difficult to hide, being easily concealed in one's clothing and brought out at the right moment.

Japanese women, especially the geishas, would conceal one or more long pins called kansashi in their hair which was worn up in a large chignon. These pins, which ranged from 5 to 6in (12–16cm) long by about 0.20in (5mm) wide, proved to be terrible and unexpected weapons capable of piercing an assailant's throat or chest.

Here, a sword attack is being parried by a jitte and a tessen held in the form of a cross.

Geishas – print by Hiroshige. Edo period. Note the large pin fixed in the chignon. If necessary, this pin (or kananshi) could become a formidable weapon.

Sai

The weapons of Okinawa: sai, tonfa, nunchaku

The sai, tonfa or nunchaku are today known as 'weapons of karate', no doubt because, the sai apart, these weapons, recently popularized by the cinema, tend to be increasingly associated with karate.

It is true that all these weapons, like karate, originated in Okinawa. They date from the 17th century when the Japanese, having conquered the island, prohibited the use of all methods of defence by the inhabitants. Gradually, new techniques evolved which could pass unnoticed. So, in *te* (or karate), agricultural implements such as the tonfa or rod for husking rice, the nunchaku or device for beating corn and the kama or sickle all became very efficient weapons.

Nowadays, these techniques have been perfected and their use paradoxically is tending to spread in Europe and the United States, much more so even than in Japan or Okinawa.

The Sai

Another traditional weapon from Okinawa: the sai, a sort of iron trident, the handle of which is protected by two hooks. Policemen used to parry sword attacks by catching the blade on the hooks. It was relatively easy to disarm the adversary or even break the blade.

Here, Master Shiokawa Terushige is engaged in a fight using a sai against an opponent armed with a sword. The contest respects the rules of chivalrous courtesy.

— Stage one: the two opponents bow to each other and remain still in order to concentrate.
— Stage two: the approach. It is a critical stage as it expresses ma-ai or the space required by each contestant.
— Stage three: the attack.
This is generally sudden and is completed in five or six movements at most. Here, although the attack is real, it is not taken to its conclusion. The weapon stops often only a hair's breadth (1 or 2mm) from the opponent's head or neck. Only affirmed masters attain such a degree of mastery.
— Stage four: the contestants part and bow to each other. They then remain quite still for a while. In spirit, the fight continues.

257

The Kusarigama, or sickle attached to a chain held down by a lead ball.
Sometimes as long as 3yds, the chain could be wrapped round the opponent's neck, foot or sword.
As for the sickle, one suspects it was used to cut off the head. This exceedingly dangerous weapon is no longer common and is only practised in a few
exceptional ryu in Japan. Here, the masters are from the Araki-Ryu.

Kusarigama

The kusarigama: sickle and chain

Of the many weapons in Japan using chains, hammers or sickles, one example is the kusarigama which has survided to this day.

The weapon consists of a chain 1 to 3yds long, held down by a ball of lead or cast iron. The chain itself is fixed to the end of a handle 20in (50cm) long with a sickle attached to the other end. The sickle is a pointed double-edged blade as sharp as a razor and used for cutting off the head.

The ninja were experts in handling this weapon which was indiscriminately used by samurai, sometimes by peasants, but more often by the police force.

Confronted by an adversary armed with a sword, the technique involves holding the sickle in one hand to threaten the opponent or parry his attacks, whilst swinging the chain with the lead ball at the end with the other hand. The skill lies in wrapping the chain round the opponent's sword, hands or feet in one quick movement. A swift action would snatch the sword from the enemy's hands or bring him down.

The metal ball could also be used to strike the head, spine or any other part of the body.

Today, some enthusiasts are still interested in the kusarigama. The sickle has been replaced by a piece of L-shaped wood, the chain by a rope and the lead ball by some inoffensive material.

The *chijiriki* is a variation of the kusarigama.

The *manrikigusari* is also a chain with a metal ball at the end but with no wooden handle or sickle. This weapon was invented

The chijiriki: a variation of the Kusarigama.
The chain is attached to the end of a rod.

The kusarigama has been adapted to make it less dangerous. A rope has replaced the iron chain and a wood sickle the iron one. Here, Master Shimizu Takagi demonstrates the art of throwing the rope with a wooden ball at the end. Aimed at the neck of a rider, it could unseat him or snatch his sword from his hands before he had a chance to use it. (*right*)

Here, Madame Shimada, Head of the Jikishin-kage Ryu, uses a wooden kusarigama in training. (*above*)

by a warrior, Masaki Toshimitsu, who guarded the main gate to Tokyo (then Edo). Wishing to defend the entrance – considered to be a holy place – without bloodshed, Masaki thought of the manrikigusari (manriki meaning 10,000 powers and kusari or gusari meaning chain).

The *kusari* or chain about 4yds long enables one to immobilize the victim as with a lasso. Folded up, it could be used to parry sharp weapons. That is why it is classified as a short arm.

Madame Shimada
watching her opponent
before attacking. (*left*)

Ninja

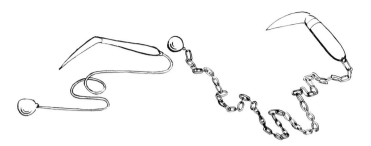

The ninja

The ninja were known throughout the centuries as dangerous men, like an early form of spy or James Bond. Their 'art' came from the idea that as they would never turn their back on any action for selfish reasons, therefore they were able to withstand extremely difficult training and were themselves capable of great sacrifice.

Although their importance is purely historical and presents a romantic image, the ninja still provide interesting food for thought.

The martial arts have nothing to do with the often criminal techniques of the ninja. However, as these techniques represented the dark side of attack and defence methods, it would be impossible to cover the martial arts without mentioning them. It is at least useful to know something about them.

The noble and magnanimous battle exploits of the samurai were not always sufficient to curb the power of the feudal lords. Spying, murder, or the elimination of embarrassing

enemies, or simply protection against spying or possible crimes, were part of the order of any established power. In Japan, the 'dirty work' was the task of a particular category of individuals: the ninja.

The origin of the ninja is uncertain. It seems to go back as far as ancient China which had already developed the science of spying. One of the greatest Chinese strategists in the field, named Sun Tzu, wrote a book of the same name: *Sun-tzu*, a book about war strategy and a sort of spy manual which seems to foreshadow the science of the ninja.

Mysterious shadow of a ninja climbing a high wall. He is gripping the slightest protrusions with the aid of a gauntlet studded with iron crampons.
Similarly, the ninja were extremely skilful at throwing ropes over walls and climbing them at speed.

In Japan itself, it was not until about 600 and especially at the end of the Heian period (1185) that the art of the ninja or ninjutsu evolved. At that time, three Yamabushi came to power in Kyoto.

Yamabushi means 'mountain warrior'. In Japan there were tens of thousands of yamabushi who, faithful to Shinto tradition, venerated the mountain and devoted at least 100 days a year to it in prayer and asceticism. The yamabushi masters developed parapsychological knowledge and techniques of resisting pain, the cold, fire, etc.

The ninja are not yamabushi. However, they too were men of the mountain, not because they venerated it but because most of them came from the steep remote mountains of the Iga and Koga regions. Cut off like wolves in these areas, they could more easily resist the different governments which, from time to time, tried to destroy them. In the

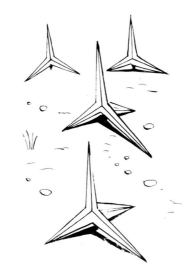

To safeguard their getaway, the ninja would scatter behind them three-sided metal spikes which would pierce the feet of their followers.

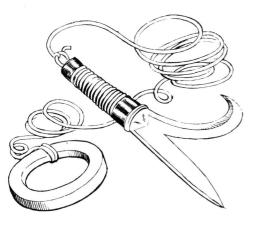

The ninja's all purpose weapon was a sort of dagger with two blades, one of which was curved and was used for hooking a rope over a wall, or for throat cutting.

home of a famous ninja from Iga, the bones of 80 corpses have been found, thrown into an oubliette by a trap door just inside the main entrance!

It is probable that the ninja themselves had a number of secrets common to the yamabushi. These secrets mainly concerned the same areas: parapsychological knowledge, resistance to pain, etc., essentially exploited by their concern for efficiency. Written in the form of a code which was indecipherable to the uninitiated, these secrets, which in modern times have been committed to the computers of the Japanese spy services, have been revealed, only to be shrouded once more in great secrecy.

In this strange world in fact, the use of parapsychological techniques is the order of the day more than ever before. The Japanese

notion of michi (or do) expressing the force of energy or intrinsic power which exists in all things, is still relevant. To capture this force, whatever its nature, offers the possibility of developing different powers, of using a great variety of hypnotic 'tricks', especially as the boundary between real power and trickery was more often than not very imprecise as far as the ninja, accomplished masters of deception, were concerned.

A ninja was neither an exceptional nor an ordinary man – rather a different sort of man, in so far as his long and very arduous training began at an early age, in childhood. He thus learnt to disjoint the bones in his body in order to squeeze through narrow railings, to climb trees like a cat, to resist cold, to hide under water by breathing through a reed, to make himself invisible or disappear behind a smoke screen and to walk noiselessly on water. In a word, all his actions were aimed at finding the point of least resistance at all levels and at using it to conquer and destroy his enemies.

The ninja's weapons are numerous: the most well-known being the shuriken, small iron devices of many different shapes such as crosses, six or eight-sided stars, triangles, pointed instruments, etc. Exceedingly sharp and with poisoned points, these weapons could silently strike an enemy from a distance. The *shuko* or sort of iron gauntlet studded with sharp points on the palm of the hand, enabled the ninja to attack sentries, to climb trees or walk on the ceiling. Armed with these gauntlets and hooked sandals, the ninja could scale walls and penetrate the most heavily defended places.

263

In order to combat their enemies, the ninja would throw different sorts of stars or iron arrows with extremely sharp edges called shuriken.

The ninja's favourite weapon was the kyotetsu-koge, a sort of dagger with two blades, one curved. It was joined to a metal ring with a rope which could be wrapped around an enemy's arm or leg, and bring him down.

Legends tell of ninja disappearing in smoke. One of their tricks in fact consisted of letting off a smoke bomb at an opportune moment and so disappearing from the enemy's sight. They also knew how to walk very fast sideways, so that they could skirt walls in the shade with their back to them in readiness for any attack.

The ninja played an important role in destroying the daimyo who opposed the tokugawa. Each side had its ninja and it is probable that the ninja could generally change camp and master according to the fortunes of the battle. Whatever happened, they were bound to absolute secrecy, on pain of violent death. Once captured, ninja sometimes managed to disfigure themselves to become unrecognizable, before committing suicide.

The ninja were divided into three groups: the *jonin,* he who makes contact and offers his services, his assistant or *chunin* and the *genin,* the actual agent who carries out the missions. The last was considered to be the lowest class of Japanese society. Once captured, he was usually tortured and dismembered.

WEAPONS FROM OKINAWA

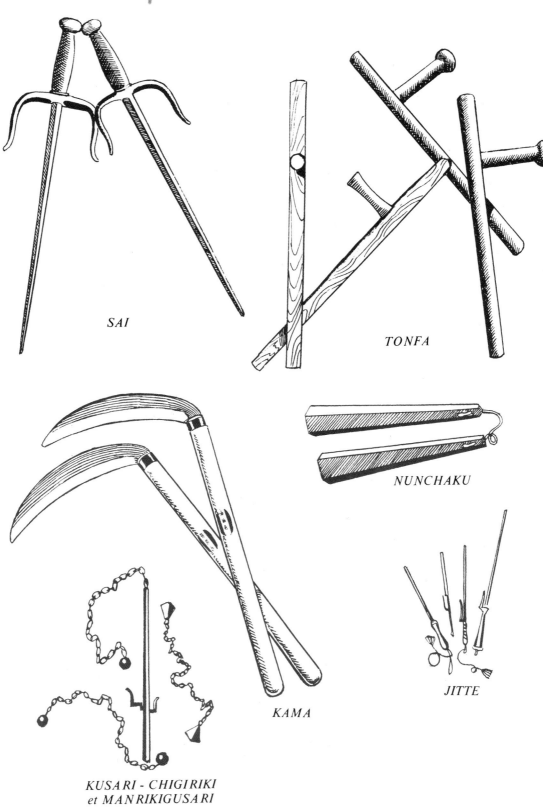

SAI

TONFA

NUNCHAKU

KAMA

JITTE

KUSARI - CHIGIRIKI
et MANRIKIGUSARI

Tonfa

Another agrarian tool transformed into a weapon, the tonfa: a rod used to husk rice, commonly known as a 'chair bar'. Here, tonfa against bo or staff, training in a dojo in Naha (Okinawa).

Kama

The sickle or kama.

Of the weapons of defence which could pass unnoticed, the sickle – or kama – used for cutting corn can be a formidable weapon.

Here, in a dojo on Okinawa, kama versus jo – or stick – in training.

Attack by kama against bo.

Kama – or sickle – kata.

Avoiding an attack from a wooden sword (bokken), the master holding the folded nunchaku in his right hand, strikes the temples.

Nunchaku

The nunchaku or cereal beater.

The nunchaku is also a weapon from the Ryukyu islands: thanks to the cinema it has regained some popularity. This weapon had been completely forgotten in Japan but is now once again taught in the dojo (especially in the West).

Here, a master from Naha (Okinawa) rolls two nunchaku in his hands during training.

How to hold the nunchaku in two hands (keep one end as low as possible).

269

The new man and the rule of the skin, flesh and bone

Throughout this book we have attempted to go further than the martial arts themselves and to capture the spirit of budo. Budo in Japanese tradition constitutes a Way equal to the greatest of Ways, reflecting all the principles – even the most esoteric, of the other more cultural Ways of nature which are: calligraphy, the art of flowers or the tea ceremony, painting, musical art and, above all, the No theatre.

Whichever Way is chosen, we find a similar approach as defined in the 15th century by Zeami, the greatest No master Japan has ever known, as the rule of the 'Skin, Flesh and Bone'.

The skin is that which is external: the surface of the body, corresponding therefore to things. In so far as I have been able to observe the artists of today', said Zeami. 'I have realized that their interpretation corresponds to the skin alone, and scarcely so . . . they are actors with an impersonal style.'[1] One can understand without difficulty that this stage is where the great majority of people stop, once formal interest (in the case of the martial arts we shall say as soon as concern for skill) takes precedence:

'I shall call flesh the appearance of the finished style which draws its strength from the study of dance and song.' Further on, Zeami explains that the skin corresponds to sight, the sense of hearing to flesh and the spirit to bone ('Then again', he says in a marginal note, 'vocal emission is skin, inflexions are the flesh, breath is bone.') The flesh appears as a stage when considerable accomplishment has been reached, for form has been surpassed, conceding to rhythm. We also find the idea expressed by Myamoto Musashi, who explains that the subtle art is knowing how to make one's own rhythm, or how to make the opponent a prison of his

[1] Quoted from René Sieffert's translation (into French) *The Traditional Secret of No* by Zeami, published (in French) by Gallimard, p. 147.

rhythm. When the form is surpassed, then the rhythm becomes the second active force. Every man who achieves rhythm in the practice of his art, knows that at that moment it is as though he is controlled and that no further effort is required of him.

'I shall call bone the existance of an innate depth and the expression of inspired power', said Zeami pointing out that rare are the actors who manage to combine these three elements. The bone is the point at which a Zen master would say that man acts by not acting. It is he who *knows* intuitively, from alpha to omega, who, according to Zeami, 'shows not the slightest sign of weakness'. Musashi said that it is the man freed of all fear and whose mastery has no further cause for expression, so strongly is this mastery felt, like an absolute force. Such was the case of Master Morihei Ueshiba who, it was said, countered his strongest adversaries by throwing them without force, almost without touching them and always with a smile on his face.

The No theatre, as seen by Zeami, is as attractive and mysterious, as complex and infinite as the Way itself. That is why he wrote:

> Forget the theatre and watch the No
> Forget the No and watch the actor
> Forget the actor and watch the idea
> Forget the idea and you will understand No.

The essence of the No theatre seems to express itself in its slowness, although according to Zeami this slowness has been progressively exaggerated, possibly to the point of being excessive. However, this slowness is concentration, the extreme slowness producing extreme quickness. 'What an expert does may seem slow', said Musashi, 'but he never departs from the rhythm.' The rhythm is the expression of fundamental energy itself; this energy is recognized as a birth, so it is beyond definition. That is why Musashi said: 'If one wants to cut swiftly with a sword, then the sword will not cut at all.'

In other words, we touch upon the fundamental principles of teachings which, while remaining secret for centuries, in Japan expressed by their profundity a similar cultural, spiritual, human and practical approach, all intermingling to form a whole, in a way which is hard to conceive nowadays.

If there is a conclusion to be drawn from this book, even at a primary level, it is to realize the extent to which ancient cultures never dissociated the essence from the form, the spirit from its expression, how the rule of the skin, flesh and bone was eventually found to be one, as inseparable as skin, flesh and bone themselves.

All contemporary crises and disputes only exist because this sovereign approach is forgotten. In fact, the atomization of cultures, 'man in pieces' as Georges Friedman said, the fragmented systematization of all functions is the void which can quickly crush our society once and for all.

The advent of the martial arts, their application on a vast scale, concern for competition, competency at any cost, so many facets are all set on a destructive course.

Apart from this there are hundreds of thousands, if not millions of young people all over the world learning judo, aiki-do, karate or kendo, etc., not all aspiring to be Bruce Lee and not all believing that the cinema and the martial arts go together; many of them learn postures which, while mastering or expressing aggression, are complex postures of concentration, meditation, self-control, thought and sometimes even more: of profound harmony and serenity. In this case, the true Spirit of budo, even if the phenomenon of the mass media is what it is, can be discovered by a large minority of people. And this minority, reflecting the widest possible range of social classes, runs the risk of being fiercely active when the time comes to confront a new generation of sound, well balanced men.

(*previous page*)
This No theatre character is called the shite. He is the only principle character of the theatre, he who performs, who acts. He is assisted by a 'waki' or supporting actor and accompanied by followers. The chorus comments, describes or relieves the shite when he has a long sequence to mime. The orchestra prepares for the actor's entrance, backs up his song or that of the chorus, and his dance rhythm. In No, everything is symbolic. Each action has a meaning. One could believe that the actor, in wearing a mask, could not express the complexity of human sentiments. But the great art of the shite lies in using his mask in such a way as to reveal the slightest emotions. Here, for instance, the shite is weeping. From the movement of his hand (holding the fan near his eyes) and the angle of the head, one can detect a profound and restrained state of suffering. The whole point of the No theatre, where everything seems artificial, is to express frames of mind and events of life in the most natural way possible.

The shite is holding a naginata. (*above*)

Glossary

Bibliography

Masters and traditions
featured in the photographic
illustrations

Ryu

Chronology of Japanese history

Glossary

Ai Love, harmony, unification.

Aiki-do 'The Way of harmony with universal energy'. Martial art developed in Japan since 1931 by Master Morihei Ueshiba. Foundation of the fist dojo, the Kobukai.
Aiki-do techniques are divided into two categories: nagewaza, throwing techniques and katame-waza, controlling techniques, 'Aikikai', the Aiki-do Association, was formed on 9 February 1948.

Aiki-jutsu Combat technique, a forerunner of aiki-do.

Amaterasu-omi kami 'The great and majestic divinity who shines in the sky'.
Sun Goddess in Shinto, Amaterasu is the daughter of a primordial couple, Izanagi and Izanami, and great great grandmother of Jinmu, the first mythical emperor of Japan.

Ashibumi First position in kyudo, or position of the feet and body in relation to the target.

Atemi A blow on the vital points of the body. Such blows could cause paralysis or even actual or supposed death.

Bo Staff measuring from 5ft to 6ft (1.60m-2m) depending on the ryu. The bo is extremely effective. The preferred weapon of the monk warriors, some ancient bo were made of iron and had a hexagonal section.

Bodhidharma The first Chan patriarch in China (460-534) and 28th patriarch after Buddha. As the story goes, he came to southern China from India in the 6th century and later settled in the Shao Lin (Shorin) temple where he trained monks in a type of unarmed combat in order to toughen their bodies and minds. The legendary part of his life is nevertheless decisive.

Bojutsu Techniques of the staff. Bojutsu is studied in the dojo as a complement to karate, kendo and aiki-do. The Japanese technique, which came from the Chinese, involves sliding the pole through the hands like a billiard cue.

Bokuseki (or calligraphy) Calligraphy is one of the Japanese martial arts. Often practised in relation to the tea ceremony. Examples of ancient calligraphy originated by the great masters are highly prized treasures in Japan.

Budo Japanese martial arts. Budo (from bu = warrior and do = the Way) means the Way of the warrior – self-defence.
Budo differs from bujutsu (from bu = warrior and jutsu = technique) in that budo belongs to a divine level (the current of the divine heart) and jutsu belongs to a human level (strength, intelligence). Bu also means reconciliation, harmony and avoiding the spear. Budo = Way of harmony or reconciliation.

Bushi Japanese warrior. The virtues of the bushi are:
— doryo = magnanimity
— shiki = resolution
— onsha = generosity, tolerance
— fudo = posture and attitude, immutability
— giri = the duty
— ninyo = magnanimity (on a different level to doryo).

Bushido 'The Way of the warrior' – code of honour of the Japanese warrior. The word, popularized by Inazo Nitobe in his work *Bushido, the Soul of Japan,* published at the beginning of this century, defines the code of honour of the ancestors: a spiritual law which Japanese nationalists in particular have constantly praised. Integrity, justice, courage, contempt of death, goodwill, politeness, sincerity, honour, loyalty and self-control are the principal rules of bushido.

Chan Form of Chinese Buddhist philosophy evolved from the Indian Dhyana and which is the origin of Japanese Zen.

Chanoyu Tea ceremony.

Chi Chinese word for vital energy, equivalent of the Japanese ki or the Hindu prana (also called qi).

Dan Master grade conferred on those who are accepted as 'initiated' (in the sense of he who knows) into one of the budo disciplines.

Do Way – spiritual path. Means both Way and object. The object is also the Way. See also *Kyuba no michi, Tao*.

Do The breastplate in kendo.

Dogen Founded the Soto sect in Zen, after studying in China (1200-53).

Dogu Tool, equipment.

Dojo School or place of training for the martial arts. Do means the Way, jo the 'place'. Dojo is the place where the Way is studied.

Dosha Grand ceremonial bowmanship (of Shinto inspiration).

Duzukuri Second position in kyudo.

Fudoshin	Imperturbable and calm spirit in the face of danger.
Fuji (Mount)	In Japan, mountains are sacred, especially Mount Fuji which is the most sacred mountain in the country. Every year thousands of people climb Fuji, many wearing white, the symbol of purity.
Funakoshi Gishin	Founder of modern karate.
Gedan	Kendo position (low guard). Also name given to the average level of the human body, from the plexus to the lower abdomen.
Geido	Artistic Way.
Genshin	Power to counter or anticipate an attack. Sort of intuition or premonition.
Go-kyo	Series of five groups of eight judo throws, each progressively more complex.
Go kui	Secrets revealed to the initiated.
Hachiman	God of war, and divine protector of Minamoto Yoritome who built a beautiful sanctuary to him in Kamakura.
Hajime	Begin: order given at the start of a contest.
Hagakure	*Hidden Beneath the Leaves,* the title of a famous work on bushido in 11 volumes, completed by Yamamoto Tsunetomo in 1716.
Hakama	Culottes worn in kendo, kyudo and aiki-do or part of Japanese traditional ceremonial costume.
Hanmi	Defence position: ready for the attack, with the body slightly inclined.
Hanshi	Higher teaching. After 8th Dan, one can become hanshi. Shihan means great master but the great master must also be hanshi and 9th Dan at least. The order of superiority is therefore renshi – kyoshi – hanshi – shihan.
Hantai	Opposed.
Hara	Stomach – centre. The hara is the region of the lower abdomen, below the navel. The Japanese consider this to be man's original centre, the psychical centre of gravity where the vital profound forces gather. The hara enables man to communicate with the primordial unity of all things. See also *Tanden*.
Hanare	Loose or releasing the arrow. Seventh kyudo position.
Hasso-no-kamae	Guard position in kendo.
Hiden	Secret tradition – arcane.
Hijutsu	Secret tradition.
Hikiwake	Fifth kyudo position: drawing the bow progressively and in stages. Also means a draw in competitions.
Hontai	Expresses mastery of the body by the mind.
Iaijutsu	Art of drawing the sword. Solitary training based on swiftness and concentration.
Ippon	Point won in a match.
Irimi	Term used especially in aiki-do to express the art of nonresistance consisting of letting the opponent's force turn against itself, however powerful. See also *Tenkan*.
Jitte	Weapon used by police in feudal times: metal rod with a prong attached to the handle. Used to check the sword. See also *Sai*.
Jo	Short stick.
Jodan no Kamae	High position in kendo: sword raised above the head.
Ju	Flexibility.
Judo	One of the martial arts, founded by Jigoro Kano (1860-1938) and evolved from jujutsu. The term judo had previously been used by the Jikishin-Ryu, but it was Kano who defined and popularized the basic principle.
Jujutsu	Unarmed combat techniques based on principles of nonresistance. Precursor of judo. (From ju: supple, weak, gentle, peaceful, yielding, succumbing; and jutsu: technique, science.)
Junshi	Custom of following one's master in death. Also mass suicide.
Kado	The Way of flowers.
Kama	Sickle, used as a weapon in Okinawa.
Kami	Shinto word meaning the gods. There are innumerable kami. A man, a waterfall, a tree, a rock can all be kami. Accomplishing one's form with harmony, assuming one's destiny whilst displaying obvious virtues, are just some of the conditions necessary to becoming a kami. Every kami is worthy of veneration.
Kamidana	Shinto family altar, ancestral worship (as opposed to butsudana, or Buddhist family altar).
Kamikaze	'Holy wind': name of the typhoon which devastated the Mongolian fleet in 1280 and name given to the suicide pilots in the last war.
Kangeiko	Special winter training in all the martial arts. For eight to ten days, training is taken to the limits of physical resistance. A similar form of training during the hottest days of summer is called shochu geiko.

Jigoro Kano	Founder of judo (1860-1938) and of the Kodokan school.
Kappo	Art of resuscitation using kuatsu (or method of reviving with the kiai).
Kabura-ya	Sort of knob shaped like a turnip attached to the ends of arrows which emits sounds intended to expel the evil spirits.
Kai	Union. Sixth kyudo position.
Kassei-ho	Means of resuscitation, particularly after strangling, using kuatsu.
Kata	Combat figures following established rules. Series of blows against imaginary opponents.
Katana	One-edged sword worn tucked in the belt, called tachi if worn suspended from the belt. It is divided into three main groups, according to length: less than 12in (30cm), tanto: dagger; 12–24in (30–61cm), shoto: short sword; over 24in (61cm), daito: great sword. A pair of swords, a long one and a short one, is called daisho.
Kawashi	Dodging.
Keiko	Training in a general sense. Kei = surpassing Ko = ancient, ancestral. Keiko also means becoming aware of the totality of the past.
Kempo	Way of the fist. Martial art of Chinese origin. In about 1600 Chinese soldiers settled in Okinawa and taught kempo to the inhabitants, who combined it with their own method. The result was a new form of combat called 'okinawa-te', the forerunner of karate.
Kendo	Originally the art of the sword. All the rules of the sword apply to kendo. However, the weapon used is called a shinai and is made of four strips of bamboo bound together. Equipment: men = mask, do = breastplate, kote = gauntlet to protect wrist and forearm.
Kenjutsu	Art of the sword, forerunner of kendo.
Ki	Energy (also known as prana-qi). Display of vital and subtle energy which exists in every man and which is no more than original energy, creator of the earth and the universe. In Japanese, the word ki means both breath and awareness. Ki is therefore energy which is fundamental to being and which, beyond physical, chemical and natural phenomena, enables one to permeate everything. Awareness itself is ki; mental force is energy and, as such, can be directed to all parts of the body or rejected. It is customary to say that ki is concentrated in the stomach (saika-tanden). In Japanese writing, the word ki is made up of signs representing the word for rice. The word rice itself is made up of ideograms meaning water and fire. In other words, cosmic energy symbolized by water and fire is concentrated in an action in order to create ki which is none other than original energy.
Kiai	A cry, concentration of ki. The opposite of aiki.
Kihon	Practice of basic movements in all budo disciplines.
Kissaki	Point of the sword or shinai.
Koan	Subtle question of the Zen sect, insolvable by reasoning. Only the state of satori (enlightenment or awakening) can bring about the solution. Phrase or image incomprehensible to the spirit – enigma acting as an aid to meditation in Rinzai Zen.
Kobudo	Ancient martial art (from ko = ancient and budo = martial art). Also used for the minor martial arts.
Kokoro	Spirit, soul, heart.
Koku	Unit for weighing rice, 317 pints (180 litres), with which the samurai were paid.
Koshi	All the internal part of the trunk of the body starting at the navel.
Kokyu	Respiration, movement of physical force, or ki, or body movement according to ki. A strong kokyu means a body with the gift of ki or of an intense psychical and spiritual energy. Communion with. The universe itself is a function of ki. Kokyu ho is the Way to manipulate others using kokyu; kokyu nage, the art of throwing others using kokyu. Fukushiki kokyu: profound abdominal respiration.
Ko-Shinto	Ancient, original Shinto.
Kote	Protective gloves used in kendo. Also a vulnerable point in kendo.
Kumite	Conventional assault in karate, corresponding to randori in judo.
Kung-fu (or gongfu)	'Human effort': generic terms for Chinese martial arts, kempo.
Kurai	A peaceful mind (like an object floating on water). Expresses the idea of a state of offering no resistance. In combat, conforming to the opponent's will until he relaxes his effort which is the moment to attack. Class or rank.
Kusari-gama	Weapon or sickle attached to a lead ball with a chain.
Kyo	Principle.
Kyuba no michi	The Way of the bow and the horse was at the end of the 12th century the first unwritten samurai law.
Kyudo	The Way of the bow.
Kyujutsu	Techniques of the bow.

Kyusho	The enemy's vital points.
Ma-ai	The distance between oneself and the opponent. The science of ma-ai consists of judging the right distance needed to establish harmony with one's partner. To penetrate the partner's ma-ai is to ensure victory.
Makimono	Scroll in the sense of diploma.
Makiwara	Straw bundle used in kyudo, karate and kendo training.
Men	Mask worn in kendo. Also a vulnerable point in kendo.
Misogi-harai	Expressing a process of purification and physical, moral and spiritual cleansing.
Muga-mushin	Annihilation of one's body and mind. Mushin, the nonintellect, as distinguished from ushin, actual intellect, in other words the intellect which concentrates on a point and becomes 'superficial'. Mushin, original intellect, knows no fixations or constrictions. It is the nonintellect which allows light to permeate.
Munen Mushin or Munen Muso	A state without thoughts or ideas.
Mushashugyo	The rovings of a knight. Going from dojo to dojo in order to increase one's knowledge and meet new partners.
Nage	Throwing technique. He who, when attacked by an adversary (tori), is thrown by him. See also *Uke*.
Naginata	Wooden halbert with an extremely sharp blade at the end. The naginata was of particular use on the battle field for hamstringing horses. Today, it is essentially a women's sport, in the form of naginata-do, but this is not true of the old ryu. An adequate translation would be 'a double-edged billhook'.
Nunchaku	Device used for beating corn, consisting of two parts joined by a short chain or rice-straw rope. Formidable weapon from Okinawa.
Okugi	Internal mysteries.
Randori	Friendly competition. Free training in judo.
Rei	Bow.
Rinzai-shu	A Japanese Zen sect, from the name of its founder (Lin Zi in Chinese).
Ronin	Out of work samurai, either through disgrace or because of the death of his master.
Roshi	Title given to a Monk Superior in Zen.
Ryu	Martial tradition.
Sado	Art of tea making.
Sai	Iron dagger protected by two lateral hooks. In particular, the sai was used as a police weapon, to check or even break a sword when attacked. (See also *Jitte*.) The sai's blade must be the exact length of the operator's forearm.
Sakura	Cherry tree. The sakura's blossom is a symbol of ephemeral beauty, unselfish love of life. It expresses the idea of death in the sense of complete detachment from life, as the cherry blossom falls from the tree of its own accord.
Samu	Concentration on manual work.
Samurai	Japanese warrior – having the right to carry two swords – top social class in Japan, the other classes being peasants, craftsmen and merchants (with the exception of the aristocracy) in that order.
Satori	Spiritual enlightenment or awakening. Word taken from Zen Buddhism. Satori is essentially an experience, a sudden awareness. An indefinable process which explains sudden enlightenment, intuitive and profound understanding of a hidden reality. Satori is not a definitive experience. In Zen, it begins with the *opening* of satori. It then continues through numerous examples of profound internal understanding – or satori.
Sen	Initiative (analysing the opponent's position). Gono-sen means expressing the idea of obstructing or counter-attacking, when one is attacked. Sen-no-sen, initiative upon initiative, or attack within attack. The idea of attacking before the opponent has launched his attack.
Sen-no-Rikyu	(1521-1571) Considered to be the greatest master of the tea ceremony (Chanoyu). The rules of his ryu (Senke) are still applied today. The tea ceremony, inspired by Zen, also interprets the spirit of wabi (see explanation) or simplicity.
Sensei	Teacher or master. Word used to express one's respect or admiration. Rather fallen into disrespect today.
Seppuku	Refined word for hara-kiri or act of suicide by disembowelment: the privilege of the samurai during feudal times.
Shado	Way of bowmanship.
Shiai	Competition, test.
Shime-nawa	Rope surrounding sacred places or things in Shinto. From Okinawa: hence the great knot, because it is the first large island one encounters on arriving in Japan.

Shingitai	The three types of grade (Dan) in the martial arts: shin = spirit, character; gi = technique in the art; tai = parts of the body. Or shin = sky; gi = earth; tai = man = combining the three elements.
Shinpan	Judge, referee.
Shinai	Bamboo sword used in kendo.
Shinobu-koi	Hidden, secret love.
Shinto	Japan's original religion, meaning 'the Way of the gods'. The word Shinto was defined as late as 560 AD in order to distinguish the earlier religious practices (until then expressed simply as 'the Way') from the growing influence of Japanese Buddhism.
Shitoryu	A karate school.
Shodo	Art of writing, calligraphy.
Shogun	Name given to the military governor of Japan prior to the Meiji era. The shogun was always invested by the emperor, and the office was frequently inherited. For centuries, the shogun had total power. Original meaning: general 'against barbarians'.
Shomen	Direct hit on the head.
Shuriken-jutsu	Art of throwing a knife.
Soto (-shu)	Japanese Zen sect founded by Dogen (1243).
Suisei-mushi	The fact of being born, living and dying in a conscious dream, which is the lot of the great majority of men. Opposed to the idea of man, part of the Great Whole.
Suki	The cerebral Void – the moment of inattention.
Sukima	The Void, absence of thought and action, the 'dead time'.
Sutemi	'Sacrifice': word used in judo and in all budo disciplines, to express the idea of throwing one's body, of surrendering one's life as if entering death, decisively and with a spirit of total sacrifice. Without 'sutemi' or totally carefree movement in attack, the ego front can bring about a defeat.
Tachi (or dachi)	Long ceremonial sword. Standing position.
Tachi-oyogi	Special martial swimming or 'standing swim', enabling one to cross a river in armour.
Tae-kwon-do	Korean karate.
T'ai-chi	The Ultimate, the supreme pinnacle.
T'ai chi-chuan	Chinese martial art, commonly called 'shadow boxing'.
Tai-sabaki	A dodge in karate and in budo. Moving the body in order to avoid an attack and using the force in action: much used in aiki-do.
Tai-wa	Yamato = Great Peace, original name of Japan: the land of the great peace.
Take	Bamboo.
Tama	The soul. In Shinto, the human soul is composed of four elements: (1) the ara-(mi) tama, or man's ability to put his ideas into practice, (2) the nigi-(mi) tama, or ability to consolidate and organize the material world, (3) the saki-(mi) tama, or ability to analyse, to divide up the world into its constituent parts, (4) the kush-(mi) tama, or ability to penetrate and unite the worlds of matter and spirit. Man's supreme achievement is his ability to combine many things in one. In Shinto, the human soul is symbolized by a helical spiral expressing universality of a Whole.
Tameshi-giri	Art of practising cutting with a sword, sword test.
Tanbo	Short staff.
Tanden	From the Buddhist conception, tanden is man's spiritual centre, situated about 0.7in (2cm) below the navel (on pictures of Buddha it is often designated by a lotus flower). All spiritual and corporal force comes from there and a basic exercise involves concentrating on the precise tension of the stomach muscles. Man's spiritual axis and centre of gravity pass through the tanden. It is the original source of 'vital' energy. A Japanese master, Sajo Tsuji, said: 'The whole art of mastering the tanden consists of this: having freed all the forces scattered throughout the body, direct and unite them in the tanden.' This art has always been taught as much in the budo (Way of the horse) as in the geido (artistic Way) and the sado (art of sitting). This point in the stomach is also called seika tanden, an expression taken from Chinese Taoism meaning 'the river of cinnabar'. It is also called kikai in Japanese, ocean of ki. See also *Hara* and *Ki*.
Tantojutsu	Dagger fighting.
Tao	Supreme essence of existence, fundamental concept of Taoism.
Taoism	The philosophy of Tao. Chinese religion traditionally founded by Lao-Tseu in the 6th century BC. *Tao-Te-King,* the principle sacred book of Taoism, is attributed to Lao-Tseu. But Tao is a word which defies exact definition. It means 'way', 'course', 'path', and many other things.
Tatami	Training mat made of compressed straw. Japanese sleeping mats.
Te	Hand.

Tenkan	Pivoting or circular movement. In aiki-do, almost all the movements are at the same time irimi and tenkan.
Tessen	Iron fan sometimes used as a weapon.
Tonfa	Technique from Okinawa. Oak rod 18–20in (45–50cm) long attached to the millstone used for pounding soya. A cylindrical handle is fixed three quarters of the way along.
Tori	The one who throws his opponent (uke) during a contest.
Tsuba	Sword and guard.
Tsuka	Handle of a sword or shinai.
Tsuki	Stab at the throat in kendo. In karate, direct attack.
Uchi	Internal. Indirect blow.
Uchiokoshi	Fourth kyudo position.
Morihei Ueshiba	Founder of aiki-do (1883-1969).
Uke	Defence, the one who submits. He who, when attacked, is thrown. See also *Nage*.
Wa	Peace. Unique Japanese expression describing the two concepts 'harmony' and 'communion': there is no word which better depicts the essence of Japanese civilization. Japan was formerly known as Yama-To, that is to say the land of the great wa wa-jin: the men of wa.
Wabi	Expresses essential poverty and simplicity. Hence, the practice of creating an object of great beauty or refinement using the simplest and cheapest materials available. Attitude expressing profound respect of the most humble elements of nature. The construction of Shinto temples and traditional Japanese wooden houses conforms to the wabi concept.
Wakaru	To be divided. To cut in two. The Chinese ideogram representing the man, the inferior, the sword. So Wakaru means a part which is simply the expression of a Whole.
Waza	Technique, skill.
Yabusame	Kyudo on horseback, nowadays a Shinto ceremony.
Yama	Mountain – ethnics, internal purification.
Yari	Spear.
Yin/yang	The Chinese word yin means all that is negative or passive, inert, lifeless, physical, dull, sinister or female. Yang is all things positive, active, expansive, moving, hard, light, luminous, male. Yin receives, yang acts. Nothing is entirely yang or yin. Yin generates yang and yang generates yin.
Yo/in (yin)	Active mind as opposed to the passive state, in (comparable to Chinese yang and yin). Positive is also called omote or irimi and negative, ura or tenkan.
Yokozuna	Large rope worn round the waist by sumo champions during festivals or ceremonies. The yokozuna is a symbol of dignity and moral integrity which is reserved for the supreme champions exclusively. In a wider sense, yokozuna means great champion.
Yoroi	Armour. At the time of the Japanese civil wars during the 16th century, a samurai's class was denoted by the type of armour worn.
Yumi	The bow.
Zanshin	Thought. Eighth and last kyudo position. Expresses the idea that the shot continues or is prolonged.
Zazen	Meditating while seated.
Zen	Discipline leading to self-realization. Zenna (or channa) in Chinese, a linguistic derivation of the sanscrit word dhyana meaning meditation.
Zendo	Place where zazen is performed.
Zenshi or Zenji	Monk superior in Zen.

Bibliography

Armstrong, Steve. *Seisan Kata of Isshinryu Karate.* Ohara Publications, 1973

Aston, William G. *Shinto: The Way of the Gods.* Scolarly, 1976

Bassett, Randall. *Zen Karate.* Warner Books, 1975

Brinkley, F. *Samurai, the Invincible Warriors.* Ohara Pubns, 1975

Bushido: The Soul of Japan. Reproduction of 1905 edition. C E Tuttle, 1969

Butler, Pat. *Judo Complete.* Faber Paperbacks, 1975

Crompton, P H. *Kung-Fu Theory and Practise.* Wehman

Dominy, Eric. *Judo: Basic Principles.* Wehman, 1975

Dominy, Eric. *Judo: Beginner to Black Belt.* Wehman

Dominy, Eric. *Judo Techniques and Tactics.* Dover, 1969

Draeger, Donn F & Nakaysma, Masatoshi. *Practical Karate.* 6 vols. C E Tuttle, 1963-65

Draeger, Donn F & Otaki, Tadao. *Kodo Kam Judo.* C E Tuttle, 1976

Draeger, Donn F & Otaki, Tadao. *Judo for Young Men.* Kodansha, 1965

Egami, Shigeru. *The Way of Karate: Beyond Technique.* Kodansha, 1976

Feldenkrais, Moshe. *Higher Judo.* Warne, 1972

Freudenberg, Karl. *Natural Weapons: A Manual of Karate, Judo, & Jujitsu Techniques.* A S Barnes, 1962

Fujisawa, Chikao. *Zen and Shinto: The Story of Japanese Philosophy.* Greenwood, 1959

Funakoshi, Gichin. *Karate — Do Kyohan: The Master Text.* Kodansha, 1973

Haines, Bruce. *Karate's History and Traditions.* C E Tuttle, 1968

Harrison, E J. *The Fighting Spirit of Japan.* Unwin, 1913 U.K.

Hawley, W M. *Shinto Bengi Oshigata.* Hawley, 1975

Herrigel, E. *Zen in the Chivalrous Art of Bowmanship.* Dervy-Livres, Paris

Hisatake, Massayuki. *Scientific Karate-do: Spiritual Development of Individuality in Mind and Body.* Japan Pubns, 1976

Holtom, D. *Modern Japan and Shinto Nationalism.* Paragon, 1963

Koizumi, C. *My Study of Judo,* Foulsham, U.K.

Kozuki, Russell. *Blackbelt Techniques in the Martial Arts.* Sterling, 1976

Mason, J W. *Shinto.* 2 vols, Gordon Pr

Mason, J W. *Meaning of Shinto.* Kennikat, 1968

Matsunga, Alicia. *Buddhist Philosophy of Assimilation.* C E Tuttle, 1969

Mitford, A B. *Tales of Old Japan.* Tuttle & Co., Tokyo, 1966

Nagai, Sinichi. *Gods of Kumano: Japan's Shinto Occult.* Kodansha, 1968

Nicol, C. *Moving Zen: Karate as a Way to Gentleness.* Morrow, 1975

Nitobe, Inatzo. *Bushido, the Warrior's Code.* Ohara Pubns, 1975

Okano, Isao & Sato, Tetsuya. *Vital Judo: Throwing Techniques.* Japan Pubns, 1973

Ono, Sokyo. *Shinto: The Kami Way.* C E Tuttle, 1962

Ratti, O & Westbrook, A. *Secrets of the Samurai: A Survey of the Martial Arts of Feudal Japan.* C E Tuttle, 1973

Seward, Jack. *Hara-Kiri: Japanese Ritual Suicide.* C E Tuttle, 1968

Shibata, Masumi. *Masters of Zen in Japan.* Maisoneuve et Larose, France, 1969

Stone, Justine F. *Bushido: Way of the Samurai.* Sun Pubns, 1975

Tai Chi Chuan. *The Philosophy of Yin and Yang and its Applications.* Ohara Pubns, 1976

Tohei, Koichi. *The Book of "Ki". Co-ordinating Body and Mind in Daily Life.* Japan Pubns, 1976

Tochei, Koichi. *Aîki-do in Daily Life.* Rikugei, Tokyo, 1966

Turnbull, Stephen. *The Samurai — A Military History.* Macmillan, 1977

Ueshiba, Kisshomaru. *Aiki-do.* Hozansha, Tokyo, 1963

Winderbaum, Larry et al. *The Martial Arts Encyclopaedia.* Inscape Corp., 1977

Yamamoto, Jocho. *The Way of the Samurai: Yukio Mishima on Hagakuri in Modern Life.* Basic, 1977

Masters and ryu illustrated in photographs

Kyudo

ANZAWA Heigiro	great master	
NAKANO	great master	
SUHARA Kazuo	great Zen master	
KITAJIMA Yoshio		
ONUMA Hideharu		

Yabusame

KANEKO Yurin	great master	

Aiki-do

UESHIBA Morihei	founder	
UESHIBA Kisshomaru	president aiki-do so honbu	Zaidan hojin aikikai
YAMAGUCHI	great master	

Karate

FUNAKOSHI Gichin	founder	
NAKAYAMA	great master	Shotokan school
NAKANO Masuomi	great master	Shorinji Kempo
SHIOKAWA Terushige	great master	
KATSUTO Mitsuhiro		Chito Ryu: Karate-Do

Naginata

SHIMADA Teruke	great master	
TERAUCHI Kenzo		Jikishin-Kage Ryu

Tameshi-giri (bamboo cutting)

NAKAMURA Taisaburo	great master	

Art of the sword (Kenjutsu)

TOMIGAHARA	great master	Shimonoseki Muso Shinden Ryu
KURODA Ichitaro	great master	
TAKANO Kosei	great master	
OTAKE Risuke	great master	Katori Ryu (Menkyo)
NODA Seizan	great master	Katori Ryu
KIKUCHI Genkichi	great master	Araki Ryu (Menkyo)

Kendo

TAKANO Kosei	great master
NIGUCHI Nobuo	great master
KAMIMOTO Eichi	great master

Judo

KANO Jigoro	founder

Sumo

TAIHO	greatest champion in the history of Sumo

The art of techniques

Kusarigama

SHIMIZU Takaji	great master (Menkyo)	
KAMINOTA Tsunemori		Maniwa-Nen
HIGUCHI Takizo	great master (Menkyo)	

The ryu or old traditions

When Emperor Meiji came to power there were a large number of ryu for the teaching of jujutsu and the art of the sword, probably at least 10,000.

Japan's old martial arts traditions, or ryu, have never been studied in depth. The secrecy which surrounds them and which still exists today allows only an outside view. Yet the ryu, most of which are scattered in country districts, have played an important role in Japan's history. Often village life centred round a ryu and its masters. Festivals, tournaments, all sorts of events involved villagers in the life of the ryu as the esoteric aspect of the teaching did not preclude a wide following.

The study of these ryu and their customs, the writing and teachings of the masters, would be a valuable source of knowledge and would lead to understanding a Japan which is both strange and fascinating. For the record, the following is a list of some of the ryu still in existence today. Note that as the old masters disappear the ryu, though centuries old in many cases, are closing down.

SWORD, NAGINATA, STAFF

Maniwa Nen Ryu	jujutsu and sword
Tenshin Shoden	
Katori-Shinto Ryu	sword, staff and naginata
Takenuchi Ryu	the founder, Hisamori Takenouchi, had a dream in June 1532 in which a Yamabushi taught him five methods of defence demonstrating the advantages of small arms over large. This art was called Kogusoku
Shinkage Ryu	sword and spear
Shindo Muso Ryu	jojutsu and sword
Jikishin-kage Ryu	naginata
Ichin Ryu	weapons with chains
Bokuden Ryu	
Tensinmegen Ryu	
Hoki Ryu	sword
Mujushin-Ken Ryu	spiritual kenjutsu (invented by Odagiri Sekiei)
Omori Ryu	sword
Araki Ryu	founded by Mataemon Araki (1594-1637) sword
Yagyu Ryu	founded by Muneyoshi Yagyu (1527-1606) the life of his son Musemori Yagyu (1571-1646) has been the subject of numerous films
Itto Ryu	single sword school founded by Kagehiso Ittosai Ito (1336-1568) Itto Ryu had a great influence on kendo
Niten-ichi Ryu	long and short swords. Miyamoto Musashi's school (1584-1645)
Tenjin Shin'yo Ryu	jujutsu combining the methods of Yoshin Ryu and Shin-no-Shindo Ryu (former masters: Yanagi Sekizai and Minamoto-no-Masatari)
Kiraku Ryu	jujutsu
Yoshin Ryu	jujutsu
Shin-no-Shindo Ryu	jujutsu
Tenjin Shinyo Ryu	jujutsu
Sekiguchi Ryu	jujutsu
Shibukawa Ryu	jujutsu
Asayami Ichiden Ryu	jujutsu
Kyushin Ryu	jujutsu
Kito Ryu	jujutsu
Ryoishinto Ryu	jujutsu
Arata Ryu	jujutsu
Shimmei Sakkatsu Ryu	jujutsu

Dan grades, titles and masters

In view of the difficulty of describing accurately the rank and exact titles of each master – and in so far as masters in the Way of the do and masters of the old traditions are grouped together – we have chosen to simplify matters by using the expression 'great master' above 7th Dan or its equivalent in the ryu.

We should add that the idea of 'great master' incorporates qualities which, in addition to perfect technical expertise, combine a humane and spiritual personality of exceptional degree. There is no actual title which expresses this dimension except possibly *O-Sensei,* or 'great teacher'.

In addition, the Dan form part of the Kyu-dan system, unique to budo (or Way of the do).

There is no defined method for awarding Dan grades. International federations which combine the different do have tried to standardize the awards while arousing opposition in some areas to such an extent that many masters no longer award Dan grades.

As for the old traditions, they have retained the system in the *bugei.* This very ancient method is based on the fact that one reflects the character of a ryu and therefore that of a master within the ryu. When one has attended a school for several years – with all that that implies as regards the close relationship between pupil and master on a technical, spiritual and human level – the master awards three to five diplomas (or makimono) up to the highest rank – menkyo (meaning master of all jutsu). All the founder masters of the do (Funakoshin, Kano and Ueshiba) attained their grades in this way. However, custom dictated that one should obtain several titles by getting to know many different ryu. Lastly, we should mention the Japanese custom of promoting a master to a higher rank when it becomes evident that a suitably qualified person has won the unanimous vote of a group of experts in the relevant discipline on account of his ability.

During the 30 years or so which witnessed the development of Budo in Japan, the really great masters in the true sense of the word were rare. Each discipline has had one of these celebrated characters of its own, for instance: in judo, Jigoro Kano; in aiki-do, Morihei Ueshiba; in karate, Funakoshi Gichin; in kyudo, the succession of masters: Kenzo Awa and Anzawa, as well as those still alive: Nakano and Masakichi Matsui; in naginata-do Shigehachi Sonobei.

Chronology of the history of Japan

BC According to legend, Jinmu Tenno, the semi-fictional emperor who claimed to be descended from the Sun Goddess, founded the imperial family in 660 BC.

AD In 238, a Chinese chronicle recorded that Wa (Japan) consisted of a number of small states governed by women. Around 300, invaders of Siberian origin, from northern Asia, settled in the country and lost no time in forming Japan's aristocracy.
Japan's frontiers spread beyond the island of Kyushu and incorporated the Yamato region on Honshu.
Japan's primitive religion grew; it was probably a form of nature worship.

About 500 Introduction of Buddhism (538 or 552). Appearance of the first Korean Buddhist art. Asuka period (552-710).

538 Spread of Buddhism and Chinese civilization and symbols. Submission of Japanese possessions in Korea (first initiative: 3rd century).

592 Regency of Prince Shotoku (died in 622).

622 Prince Shotoku's Constitution in 17 clauses. He encouraged Buddhism.

646 Reform during the Taika era, along the lines of the Chinese Tang Dynasty. The object of this reform was the reunification of Japan.

663 Japanese expelled from Korea.

710-84 Nara period from the name of the first permanent capital.

712 Collection of all Japan's ancient documents – mythology and legends – into single works: *The Kojiki* (the 'Bible of Shinto') and the *Nihon Shoki* (720).

749 Inauguration of the Great Buddha in Nara.

794 Capital moved to Kyoto (Heian Kyo).

794-857 First Heian period.

841 The power of the Fujiwara began to assert itself.

857-1160 **Fujiwara period.**

858 The Fujiwara family remained in control by dominating the regents for the first time.

894 Abolition of regular missions with China in order to accelerate the development of the new culture.

1185 Conflict between the Taira and Minamoto clans ending in victory for the latter.
Minamoto Yoritomo began to found a regime based on the samurai code of loyalty; he rewarded faithful vassals with positions of importance.
Kamagura became the general seat of Yoritomo's military dictatorship.

1192 Yoritomo appointed shogun of Japan.
On the death of Yoritomo, the Hojo regents managed to dominate the shogunate.

1200 Introduction of Zen from China.

1225 Eisai the monk founded a school for Zen Buddhism in Japan; the Zen school, encouraged by Dogen, was very popular with the samurai and feudal lords.

1274-81 The Mongols' first and second attempts to invade. The invasion forces of Kublai Khan, the Mongol emperor from China, landed on Kyushu; after an inconclusive battle, a storm scattered the invaders' ships.
In 1281, the Mongols again tried to invade Japan but failed because a typhoon sank their fleet.

1318-38 Revival of imperial power (Go-Daigo). Story of the Heike and other war accounts of the Kamakura period very popular.

1333 Emperor Go-Daigo destroyed Kamakura. The last of the Hojo regents committed suicide.
Ashikaga Takauji replaced Go-Daigo with a puppet emperor and governed the state from his Kyoto residence. Go-Daigo established a rival court south of the capital.

1338 Ashikaga Takauji became shogun but the conflict between the two rival courts continued for about half a century (from 1336 until 1392).

1401 New ties with China.

1410 Birth of the No theatre codified by Zeami (1363-1456).

1450-1500 Golden age of Fine Arts (painting, architecture, gardens) known as the Higashiyama era.

1467-77 Feudal war of the Onin period. Annihilation of numerous families.

1477 Civil war. Collapse of central power. The Ashikaga shoguns lost all their power. The imperial house on its last legs.

1532 Civil war.

1543 First contact with the West. Portuguese merchants entered Japan through Kyushu and introduced fire arms.

1549 Arrival in Japan of the Spanish missionary St Francis Xavier.

1560 Nobunaga defeated an army led by the Daimyo Imagawa and became Japan's first warrior.

1568 Nobunaga occupied Kyoto and controlled the centre of Japan. Nobunaga declared war on the Buddhist sects, destroyed monasteries and the religious centre of Mount Hiei.

1573-82 Rule of Oda Nobunaga (1534-82). End of the Ashikaga shogunate. Political order and unity.

1571 Nobunaga destroyed the fortified monasteries and crushed the religious revolts.

1575 Fire arms used against swords. At the battle of Nagashino in which samurai from the Takeda lands fought the Daimyo Oda Nobunaga, the latter equipped an army of 300 intrepid peasants with muskets and overthrew the samurai. This defeat in which fire arms opposed side arms, signalled the end of the samurai.

1582 Nobunaga's assassination.
Hideyoshi succeeded him and formulated a repressive legislation which was to enforce strict feudal structures on Japan.

1587	Expulsion of missionaries and ban on Christianity. The tea ceremony codified by Sen no Rikyu.
1590	Hideyoshi subdued the last of his opponents and ruled over a unified Japan.
1592-98	Hideyoshi failed in his attempt to invade Korea. Death of Hideyoshi in 1598.
1597	Second edict against Christians.
1600	Tokugawa Ieyasu, founder of the Tokugawa shogunate, succeeded Hideyoshi. He defeated the rebellious Daimyo at the battle of Sekigahara and became master of Japan; he transferred the seat of the shogunate from Kyoto to Edo.
1603	Ieyasu shogun. Power of the Tokugawa
1615	Ieyasu, master of Japan following the Osaka victory.
1637-39	Revolt and persecution of the Christians in Shimabara. The Portuguese expelled in retaliation and Japan's doors closed to foreign influence. The majority of missionaries left Japan but some went underground. Period of intense persecution during which thousands of Japanese Christians were martyred. (There were about 700,000 Christians).
1657	Great Fire of Edo.
1673	Failure of England's attempts to trade with Japan.
1701	The 47 ronin.
1716	Yoshimune, eighth shogun. Poor economic climate. Social tension. Yoshimune attempted to remedy a hopeless situation.
1745	Ieshige, ninth shogun.
1760	Ieharu, tenth shogun.
1786	Ienari, eleventh shogun.
1783-87	Bad rice harvest. Serious epidemics and famine. Revolts. Prime minister Matsudaira Sadanobu's attempts at economic and social reform. Rebirth of Shinto movements, drawing attention to the rights of the imperial dynasty. Opposition to the shogunate.
1838	Famine. Threats of economic collapse.
1846	With warships in Uraga, the Americans invited Japan to sanction foreign trade. Japan refused.
1853	Iesada, thirteenth shogun. The American squadron commander (Commodore Perry) invited the government to open up her ports, saying that he would come for a reply the following year.
1854	Return of Perry and signing of the first treaty with the United States. Japan emerged from her isolation.
1857	End of official persecution of the Christians.
1858	Signing of a trade agreement with the United States which the emperor refused to ratify.
1863	Iemochi, fourteenth shogun. Bombing of Kagoshima by the British fleet as a reprisal.
1864	Reprisals against Japan: forts on Choshu destroyed by Dutch, French and British warships.
1866	Yoshinobu (Keiki): fifteenth and last shogun.
1868-1912	**Meiji era.** End of the shogunate. Return of power to the emperor.
	Accession of Mutsu-Hito to the throne under the name Meiji. The court established in Edo and its name changed to Tokyo.
1869	Ports opened up. End of feudal resistance in Hakodate.
1871	Samurai stripped of their privileges. Beginning of the colonization of Hokkaido.
1874	Modern reforms. Abolition of the feudal system. First people's assembly.
1876	The carrying of two swords prohibited.
1877	Satsuma rebellion (samurai revolt led by Saigo Takamori, against the emperor's desire to modernize Japan). In revolting, the samurai preferred to use their traditional weapons and forbad the use of fire arms which they never the less possessed. They were defeated by an army of conscripts from mixed social classes, constituting Japan's first modern army, so putting an end to the samurai once and for all.
1889	Formal proclamation of the Constitution.
1894-95	Sino–Japanese war ending in victory for the Japanese.
1904-05	Russo–Japanese war: another Japanese victory.
1910	Japan annexed Korea.
1912	**Taisho era.** Death of Emperor Meiji. Accession of Yoshi-Hito.
1914	Japan joined in the First World War on the side of the allies.
1921	Hiro-Hito's Regency.
1923	Tokyo's great earthquake.
1926	**Showa era.** Death of Emperor Yoshi-Hito. Accession of Emperor Hiro-Hito.
1930	Population of Japan 64,450,000, having doubled itself in a century.
1931	Japanese quest for trade outlets in China.
1933	Japanese withdrawal from the League of Nations.
1936	Attempt at a 'second restoration' by young army officers.
1937	Start of military intervention in China.
1940	Signing of an alliance (tripartite agreement) with Germany and Italy.
1941	July: occupation of Indo-China. December: Japanese attack on Pearl Harbour. Japan entered the Second World War.
1941-42	Japanese victories in Asia and the Pacific. Naval battle in the Coral Sea.
1942	Midway Islands defeat.
1942-44	Fall of the Tojo cabinet. Bombing of Tokyo. December 1944: Russia declared war on Japan.
1945	January: repossession of the Philippines by the Americans. April-June: Okinawa. Occupation of the Ryukyu islands by the Americans. Early August: atomic bombs dropped on Hiroshima and Nagasaki. 13 August: bombing of Tokyo. 15 August: Japan's defeat acknowledged in a message from the emperor. 2 September: Japan's surrender on board the 'Missouri'.
1945-52	American occupation of Japan.
1947	New Constitution.

1951 Japanese–American security treaty and San Francisco peace treaty. End of the occupation.

1956 Japan's entry to the United Nations.

1960 Riots provoked by the renewal of the Japanese–American security treaty.

1964 Sato Eisaku, tenth prime minister since the war. Constitutional changes. Olympic Games in Tokyo.

1970 EXPO 70, international fair held in Osaka. Japanese economy booming.

1972 Prime Minister Kakuei Tanaka signed peace treaty with China. Japan severed relationships with Taiwan.

1972 Self-defence forces, formerly a police reserve, numbered 250,000 men.

1974 Population reached 110,050,000.

1977 Prime Minister Takeo Fukuda took power for the Liberal Democratic Party.

By the same author, published by Denoël

Les Puissances du Dedans (*The Internal Powers*)
(essays) 1966

Le Grand Jeu (*The Great Game*)
(essays) 1970

Many friends and helpers have assisted in the preparation of this book. I
am particularly grateful to: Louis Frédéric for re-reading the manuscript,
also Jean-Lucien Jazarin, President of the College of Black Belts, Jacques
Delcourt, President of the European Karate Union, Claude Hamot,
President of the National Kendo Committee, Michel Martin (kyudo),
Bernard Le Dauphin (swords and armour), Christian Cervenansky and
Louis Renelleau (judo photos), Master Noro (aiki-do), André Nocquet,
Master of Aiki-do for the photos of Master Ueshiba, Roland Habersetzer
(karate diagrams), as well as Donn Draeger for his kind cooperation in
Japan.
I should also like to express my profound gratitude to the many Japanese
masters named below:

AIKI-DO
Kisshomaru Ueshiba
Seigo Yamaguchi

ART OF THE SWORD
Risuke Otake
Takaji Shimizu
Genkichi Kikuchi
Takizo Higughi
Tomigahara
Ichataro Kuroda
Taizaburo Nakamura
Kasegai Takashi
Tsunemori Kaminota
Terushige Shiokawa

KENDO
Kosei Takano
Eichi Kamimoto
Nobuo Higuchi

NAGINATA
Madame Teruke Shimada
Kenzo Terauchi

KARATE
Terushige Shiokawa
Masuomi Nakano

KYUDO
Heigiro Anzawa
Kazuo Suhara
Hideharu Onuma

YABUSAME
Yurin Kaneko